AF225979

Numerology Workbook

Decode Your Life Path, Uncover Your Soul's Blueprint, and Unlock the Power of Numbers to Transform Your Future

Your Free Gift
(only available for a limited time)

Thanks for getting this book! If you want to learn more about various spirituality topics, then join Mari Silva's community and get a free guided meditation MP3 for awakening your third eye. This guided meditation mp3 is designed to open and strengthen ones third eye so you can experience a higher state of consciousness. Simply visit the link below the image to get started.

https://spiritualityspot.com/meditation

Or, Scan the QR code!

Table of Contents

Overall Introduction:
Connect Logic and Pattern Recognition

Numbers are the foundation of logic. They provide a framework for the physical laws that govern our existence. When you look at a clock or a bank statement, you see the practical application of math. But numbers also describe the cycles of the human experience. This workbook treats numerical data as a tool for self-assessment. You will use basic arithmetic to gain clarity about your character and your future.

Humans have an innate drive to find patterns. We look at the stars and see constellations. We look at market data and see trends. This is not a coincidence. A study by **Dr. Mark Mattson** at the **National Institute on Aging** shows that human intelligence relies heavily on pattern recognition. This cognitive ability allows us to predict outcomes and make better choices. This book applies that same logic to your personal data. Your birth date and the letters in your name are the primary data points.

The Biological Basis of Pattern Recognition

Our brains function as sophisticated pattern-matching machines. This is a survival trait. In the wild, recognizing the pattern of a predator's stripes could save a life. In the modern era, we use this same neural circuitry to process information. **Stanislas Dehaene**, a neuroscientist and author of *The Number Sense*, argues that humans have an evolutionary "accumulator" for numbers. We are born with the ability to perceive quantities. We use this biological foundation to build language, science, and social structures.

When you start to look at your life through numbers, you are not inventing something new. You are using a built-in mental tool. You are taking the raw data of your life and organizing it. This process helps you see connections that were previously hidden. It moves you away from emotional reactions and toward logical analysis.

Data analysis is the primary way we make sense of our surroundings. When you see a red light, you know it signifies "stop." This is a learned pattern. When you see a sequence of numbers like 2, 4, 6, 8, your brain automatically predicts that 10 is next. This is linear progression. This workbook uses these same logical progressions to help you see where your life is headed.

The Historical Foundations of Numerical Frameworks

The use of numbers to define the self is not a new concept. It dates back to the earliest civilizations. The Babylonians used base-60 math to track time and the movements of the planets. They saw that celestial patterns repeated. They believed that these repetitions influenced life on Earth.

In ancient Greece, **Pythagoras** took these ideas further. He is often called the father of mathematics. Most people know him for the Pythagorean theorem in geometry. However, his work went much deeper. He taught that "all is number." He believed that the entire universe could be expressed through mathematical ratios.

Pythagoras founded a school where students studied four branches of science: arithmetic, geometry, music, and astronomy. He called this the **Quadrivium**. He argued that music was just "applied number." A string on a lyre produces a specific sound based on its length. If you halve the length, the pitch rises by an octave. This is a mathematical certainty. Pythagoras applied this same logic to human character. He believed that people also have "vibrations" or frequencies that we can measure with numbers.

He saw that the numbers 1 through 9 represented a complete cycle of growth. This cycle repeats in everything from the phases of the moon to the development of a human cell. By using the Pythagorean system, we can categorize human traits into these nine stages. This provides a repeatable and objective way to study personality.

The Mathematics of Nature: Fibonacci and Chaos Theory

Nature operates in cycles. We see this in the change of seasons and the tides of the ocean. In biology, we study **circadian rhythms**. These are internal clocks that regulate sleep, hunger, and hormone levels. If your internal clock is out of sync with your environment, your health suffers.

Mathematics allows us to track these rhythms. For example, the **Fibonacci sequence** appears throughout nature. This sequence is a series of numbers where each number is the sum of the two preceding ones: 0, 1, 1, 2, 3, 5, 8, 13, and so on. You find this pattern in the arrangement of seeds in a sunflower. You see it in the spiral of a pinecone. This is known as **phyllotaxis**, and it is the most efficient way for plants to pack seeds or leaves.

If the physical world follows these strict mathematical paths, it is logical to assume that human lives do too. This workbook uses these cycles to help you plan. You will learn to identify which "season" of life you are in. This helps you know when to push forward and when to wait.

We also look at **Chaos Theory**. This branch of mathematics deals with complex systems. It shows that even in systems that appear random, there are underlying patterns and feedback loops. Your life might feel messy, but it usually follows a specific trajectory based on your core data. By identifying your numbers, you find the "attractor" or the central point that your life revolves around.

The Psychology of Quantifying the Self

Many people struggle with self-improvement because their goals are too vague. They want to be "happier" or "more successful." These words are subjective. They mean different things to different people. Numbers provide a fixed scale. They do not change based on your mood.

By converting your name and birth date into numerical values, you create a baseline. This is similar to a doctor taking your blood pressure or checking your heart rate. It provides a data point. Once you have that data, you can make informed changes.

A 2015 study published in the journal *Psychological Science* found that people who use structured self-tracking tools are more likely to reach their goals. This is often called the **Quantified Self** movement. The act of measuring something changes how you interact with it. When you track your personal numbers, you become an active participant in your development. You stop guessing and start calculating.

This approach also leverages **Self-Verification Theory**. Proposed by **William Swann**, this theory suggests that people have a strong desire to confirm their existing self-views. When you see your traits reflected in numerical data, it provides a sense of coherence. It validates your experiences. This validation is a strong motivator for change.

The Evolution of Numerical Thought

To see why numbers matter, we must look at how we developed them. Early humans used tally marks on bones. These marks tracked lunar cycles or the number of animals in a herd. This was the birth of data storage. By recording numbers, humans could plan for the winter. They could share resources fairly. Numbers were the first tool for civilization.

As societies grew, numbers became more abstract. The Indians and Arabs developed the decimal system and the concept of zero. This allowed for complex commerce and engineering. Without these numbers, we could not build skyscrapers or fly planes. We use these same abstract tools to build a map of your personality.

In the 17th century, **Gottfried Wilhelm Leibniz** developed binary code. This uses only 1s and 0s to represent all information. Today, every piece of technology you use runs on this simple numerical logic. Your phone, your computer, and your car are all driven by sequences of numbers. This workbook suggests that you are also driven by a numerical code. Your birth date and name are your input data. The result is your current life experience.

Scientific Evidence for Synchronicity and Probability

We must look at the work of **Carl Jung** and **Wolfgang Pauli**. Jung was a psychologist, and Pauli was a Nobel Prize-winning physicist. Together, they studied **synchronicity**. This is the idea that events can be "meaningfully related" even if they do not have a direct cause-and-effect link. They believed that the universe has an underlying order that we can perceive through patterns.

Probability is another mathematical field that applies here. Statistics show that certain events are more likely to happen during specific windows of time. For example, the **Pareto Principle**, or the 80/20 rule, shows that 80% of results often come from 20% of efforts. This is a mathematical law of efficiency. This workbook helps you find your "20%." It identifies the specific times and areas where your efforts will yield the most results.

The Impact of Frequency and Vibration

In physics, everything has a frequency. This includes light, sound, and matter. **Max Planck**, the founder of quantum theory, stated that all matter originates and exists only by virtue of a force which brings the particles of an atom to vibration. If matter is vibration, then numbers—which measure frequency—are the descriptions of that matter.

When we speak of a number's "vibration," we are talking about its specific qualities. A "1" has a different frequency than a "9." This is similar to how different colors of light have different wavelengths. Red light has a long wavelength and low frequency. Violet light has a short wavelength and high frequency. They are both light, but they behave differently. Numbers act the same way. This workbook helps you identify which frequencies are dominant in your life. You can then learn how to tune your actions to those frequencies for better results.

Why Logic Supersedes Emotion in Planning

Emotional decisions are often unreliable. You might feel confident today and fearful tomorrow. If you make a major life choice based on a temporary feeling, you may regret it later. Logic provides a steady hand.

Consider the "Magical Number Seven." In 1956, psychologist **George A. Miller** published a paper showing that the human brain can hold about seven pieces of information in its short-term memory. This is a biological limit. When you have too many choices, your brain shuts down. This is called **analysis paralysis.**

Numerology simplifies your choices. Instead of looking at a thousand different career paths, you look at the three or four that align with your Life Path number. This reduces the cognitive load. It allows you to focus your energy on a specific target. You move from a state of overwhelm to a state of directed action.

The Role of Names in Human Identity

Your name is more than just a label. It is a set of sounds that you hear every day. In linguistics, the **bouba/kiki effect** shows that humans associate certain sounds with specific shapes or traits. We have a biological reaction to the phonetics of a name.

The Pythagorean system converts these phonetic vibrations into numbers. This allows us to quantify the impact of your name on your life. We look at the vowels to find your internal drivers. We look at the consonants to see your external image. By doing this, you can see if your name is helping you or holding you back. Some people find that their nicknames or married names change their numerical profile. This workbook will show you how to analyze those changes.

Cognitive Reframing Through Numerical Data

One of the most useful parts of this workbook is the ability to reframe your past. Most people view their failures as personal flaws. They think they did something wrong. When you look at your cycles, you might see that you were simply in a "9" year. A "9" year is a time for endings and letting go. It is not a time for growth or new starts.

By seeing this pattern, you stop blaming yourself. You realize that you were simply working against the current cycle. This is called **Cognitive Reframing**. It is a core technique in **Cognitive Behavioral Therapy (CBT)**. It involves changing the way you look at an event to change how you feel about it. Numbers provide the evidence you need to reframe your life story in a way that is logical and helpful.

Managing Expectations with Data

This workbook is not a crystal ball. It does not predict exactly what will happen to you. Instead, it predicts the *nature* of the events you will face. Think of it like a weather forecast. If the forecast says it will rain, you should bring an umbrella. The forecast does not tell you exactly where every raindrop will fall. It tells you the general conditions so you can prepare.

Preparation is the key to success. **Louis Pasteur** said, "Chance favors the prepared mind." When you know your numbers, you are prepared for the "weather" of your life. You know when to be aggressive and when to be cautious. This data-driven approach removes the anxiety of the unknown.

The Global History of Numerology

While we focus on the Pythagorean system, it is important to know that numbers have been used this way all over the world.

- **The Chaldeans** in ancient Mesopotamia developed one of the oldest systems.
- **The Chinese** use the *I Ching*, which is based on 64 hexagrams of binary logic.
- **The Hebrews** used *Gematria*, where each letter of the alphabet has a numerical value used to find deeper meanings in texts.

This global use shows that the logic of numbers is a universal human experience. It transcends culture and language. It is a shared tool for making sense of the world. By using this workbook, you are participating in a tradition that spans thousands of years.

Understanding the Three-Book Structure

This workbook is a comprehensive system. We have organized it into three books to help you build your profile step by step.

Book 1: Decode Your Life Path

This is your foundation. Your birth date is a fixed point in time. It creates your Life Path number. This number tells you about your natural character and the lessons you are here to learn. We look at the single digits 1 through 9. We also cover Master Numbers 11, 22, and 33. These are higher-octave versions of the single digits and require specific handling.

Book 2: Uncover Your Soul's Blueprint

Once you have your foundation, we look at your expression. This comes from your name. You will calculate your Heart's Desire, your Personality number, and your Expression number. This helps you find the balance between who you are on the inside and who you appear to be to the world.

Book 3: Unlock the Power of Numbers to Transform Your Future

The final book puts your data into motion. You will learn about the Nine-Year Cycle. You will calculate your Personal Year and Month. This is the strategic part of the workbook. You will use this information to create a five-year plan. You will also learn about relationship compatibility.

How to Achieve Best Results

To get the most value from this book, you must be precise.

1. **Use your birth certificate:** Do not guess your birth name or date. Use the official records.

2. **Do the math twice:** Simple addition errors are common. Always double-check your work.

3. **Keep a journal:** Record your calculations and your thoughts in the workbook sections.

4. **Be honest:** When reading the descriptions of the numbers, look at your weaknesses as well as your strengths.

This is a process of self-audit. The more accurate your data, the more helpful the results will be. Treat this like a scientific experiment where you are the observer and the subject.

The Ethics of Numerical Data

Using numbers for self-improvement is a responsibility. This data is for your personal growth. It is not meant to be used to judge or control others. While we look at compatibility in Book 3, the goal is always to improve communication, not to limit your social circle.

Data should be used to expand your options, not restrict them. If your numbers suggest you are not naturally suited for a specific career, that does not mean you cannot do it. It simply means you will have to work harder in certain areas. Knowledge of your numbers gives you the choice to adapt.

Final Instructions Before Beginning

You are ready to start. The first step is to clear your mind of any preconceived notions about your personality. Let the numbers tell the story. Approach the math with curiosity.

We will start with Book 1. We will define the framework of numerical influence and find your Life Path. This is the most important calculation you will make. It sets the stage for everything else.

The logic is simple. The patterns are clear. The data is yours. Let us begin.

BOOK ONE:
Decode Your Life Path

Introduction:
Define the Framework of Numerical Influence

A framework is a support structure. In architecture, it is the skeleton that holds a building upright. In the study of human behavior, a framework is a set of rules or data points that help us categorize actions. This first Book focuses on your birth date as the primary framework for your life. Why do we start with your birth date? We start here because your birth date is the first piece of data ever recorded about you. It is a fixed point that never changes. It serves as the anchor for your entire profile.

The Science of Temporal Landmarks

Psychologists have studied how specific dates affect human psychology. **Dr. Katy Milkman** at the **Wharton School** has conducted extensive research on "temporal landmarks." These are dates that stand out from the ordinary flow of time. Examples include New Year's Day, birthdays, or the start of a new week. These landmarks create a "fresh start effect." They allow people to separate their past selves from their current goals.

Your birth date is the ultimate temporal landmark. It is the moment you began your existence within the framework of human society. This date is not random. It places you within a specific year, month, and day in the Gregorian calendar. This placement determines the cycles you will face throughout your life. By defining this framework, you can see how your life moves in a predictable pattern.

Is it possible that a simple date influences your personality? Research suggests that it is. A study conducted at **Semmelweis University** in Budapest found that the season of your birth has a measurable impact on your mood. Researchers analyzed over 400 subjects and linked birth seasons to specific neurotransmitter levels. For example, people born in the summer often show more frequent mood swings. Those born in the winter are less likely to be irritable. This provides a biological basis for the idea that the timing of your birth creates a framework for your temperament.

The Physics of Resonance and Synchronization

To understand numerical influence, we must look at the physics of resonance. In 1665, the Dutch scientist **Christiaan Huygens** discovered a phenomenon called "entrainment" or "synchronization." He noticed that two pendulum clocks hanging on the same wall would eventually swing in perfect unison. They synchronized through tiny vibrations in the wood. This is a fundamental law of physics.

Numbers represent these vibrations. Every date has a specific frequency. When you were born, you were "entrained" to the frequency of that specific day. This frequency becomes your baseline. It is the "pendulum" that sets the pace for your life. When you calculate your Life Path number, you are identifying your primary frequency. You are finding the rhythm that your life naturally follows.

How does this frequency affect your daily life? It influences your natural preferences. Some people are naturally drawn to high-energy environments. Others prefer quiet and solitude. This is not just a personality quirk. It is a result of your internal frequency being in or out of sync with your surroundings. When you understand your framework, you can choose environments that match your natural resonance.

The Gregorian Calendar as a Logical System

We use the Gregorian calendar to calculate our numbers. This calendar is a mathematical model of the Earth's orbit around the sun. It is a precise tool. It uses leap years to ensure that our dates stay aligned with the seasons. Because this system is so accurate, it provides a stable source of data.

History shows that humans have always used calendars to organize their behavior. The ancient Egyptians used the rising of the star Sirius to predict the flooding of the Nile. This allowed them to plan their agriculture. They were using a numerical framework to survive. You are doing the same thing. You are using the numerical framework of your birth date to plan your career, your relationships, and your personal growth.

The numbers 1 through 9 form the basis of this system. These numbers represent a complete cycle of energy. Think of it like a musical scale. There are seven basic notes in an octave. After the seventh note, the cycle repeats at a higher frequency. Numerology follows a similar nine-step cycle. Every human life moves through these stages. Your Life Path number tells you which stage is your "home base."

The Law of Small Numbers in Personality Assessment

When we look at numbers, we must be careful not to fall into the "Law of Small Numbers." This is a cognitive bias identified by psychologists **Amos Tversky** and **Daniel Kahneman**. It describes the tendency for people to draw broad conclusions from a small amount of data. For example, if you meet one person with a Life Path 5 who is impulsive, you might assume all 5s are impulsive.

To avoid this bias, this workbook uses a comprehensive data set. We do not just look at one number. We look at how your Life Path interacts with your name and your cycles. However, the Life Path is the most important part of the framework. It provides the broadest context for your life. It is the "big picture" data.

Kahneman's work in *Thinking, Fast and Slow* explains that our brains use "heuristics" or shortcuts to make decisions. Numerology provides a logical heuristic. Instead of feeling overwhelmed by the infinite possibilities of your personality, you can focus on the core traits associated with your number. This provides mental clarity. It allows you to move from "System 1" thinking (fast and emotional) to "System 2" thinking (slow and logical).

The History of the Pythagorean School

The framework we use today comes from the school of **Pythagoras**. He was more than just a mathematician. He was a philosopher who believed that numbers were the building blocks of reality. He taught his students that numbers have "qualitative" properties as well as "quantitative" ones.

A quantitative property is what we use in math: $1 + 1 = 2$. A qualitative property is the *character* of the number. For Pythagoras, the number 1 represented the "Monad." It stood for unity, leadership, and the beginning of all things. The number 2 was the "Dyad," representing duality, balance, and partnership.

His school was the first to create a structured system for analyzing character through numbers. They believed that by understanding the numbers in a person's life, you could understand their "soul's music." This idea of "The Music of the Spheres" suggested that the planets, the stars, and human beings all moved to a mathematical rhythm. By identifying your Life Path, you are finding your part in that universal music.

Defining Your Path vs. Your Personality

It is important to distinguish between your Life Path and your personality. Your personality is how you act. It can change based on your mood, your environment, or who you are with. Your Life Path is where you are going. It is the destination.

Think of it like a road trip. Your personality is the car you drive. It might be a fast sports car or a reliable truck. Your Life Path is the highway you are on. If your Life Path is a "7," you are on the "Highway of Knowledge." No matter what car you drive, your destination is the same. You are here to learn and analyze. Understanding this distinction helps you stop trying to change the highway and start focusing on how to drive your car more effectively.

Are there obstacles on this highway? Yes. Every number has its challenges. A "4" Life Path will face obstacles related to work and structure. An "8" Life Path will face obstacles related to power and money. These challenges are part of the framework. They are not mistakes. They are the specific "lessons" built into your numerical code. By identifying them early, you can prepare for them.

The Role of Probability in Personal Success

Success is often a matter of being in the right place at the right time. This is a mathematical reality. In the book *Outliers*, author **Malcolm Gladwell** discusses how the birth months of professional hockey players affect their success. In Canada, the eligibility cutoff for youth hockey is January 1st. Children born in the first few months of the year are older and physically more developed than their peers. They get more coaching and more ice time. Over ten years, this small mathematical advantage turns into a massive professional gap.

Numerology applies this same logic to your life. When you know your Life Path, you know your "eligibility." You know which fields and activities you are naturally "older" or more developed in. If you are a "3" Life Path, you have a natural advantage in communication. If you ignore this and try to work as a silent data entry clerk, you are wasting your mathematical advantage. You are playing a game where the rules are stacked against you.

Knowing your framework allows you to play the games where you have the best odds of winning. It allows you to align your career and hobbies with your natural talents. This is the most efficient way to live. It reduces friction and increases your chances of reaching your goals.

The Biological Reality of Cycles

We cannot talk about numerical frameworks without talking about biology. Every cell in your body follows a cycle. **The Hayflick Limit** is a scientific concept that shows human cells can only divide a certain number of times before they stop. This is a numerical limit on biological life.

Our bodies also follow **septenary cycles**. Every seven years, almost every cell in your body has been replaced. You are literally a different person every seven years. This seven-year cycle is a mathematical framework for physical growth. Numerology uses a similar nine-year cycle for emotional and spiritual growth. By understanding these cycles, you can see that change is not only possible but inevitable.

When you feel stuck, it is often because you are at the end of a cycle. You are trying to hold onto something that is naturally concluding. Or, you might feel impatient because you are at the beginning of a cycle and want immediate results. Understanding the framework of cycles gives you patience. It allows you to see that your life is moving according to a plan, even when you cannot see the finish line.

Quantitative Self-Observation

This workbook encourages a practice called **Quantitative Self-Observation**. This is the act of using data to track your own behavior. It is a common technique in modern behavioral science. By recording your numbers and comparing them to your daily experiences, you become a scientist in your own life.

This process removes the emotion from self-criticism. Instead of saying "I am a failure at relationships," you look at the data. You might see that your Life Path 1 (independence) is clashing with your partner's Life Path 2 (dependence). This is not a personal failure. It is a numerical clash. Once you see the data, you can solve the problem logically. You can find ways to balance those two frequencies.

Does this mean your life is predetermined? No. Numbers provide the framework, but you provide the action. Think of your Life Path as the rules of a game. If you are playing chess, the pieces can only move in certain ways. You cannot move a pawn like a queen. However, within those rules, there are an infinite number of moves you can make. The better you understand the rules, the better you will play the game.

The Impact of Social Frameworks

We also live within social numerical frameworks. Our tax IDs, social security numbers, and bank account numbers define our place in the economy. These numbers are used by institutions to track and manage large populations.

Numerology suggests that there is a deeper, personal framework that exists beneath these social numbers. While your tax ID tells the government about your money, your Life Path tells you about your purpose. Both are important for navigating the modern world. One helps you handle your external life, and the other helps you handle your internal life.

By identifying your internal framework, you become less susceptible to external pressure. You stop trying to fit into the frameworks that society has built for you and start building a life that fits your own data. This is the ultimate goal of Book 1. We want to strip away the "noise" of social expectations and find the "signal" of your true path.

The Importance of Precision in Data Entry

As you move through the chapters of Book 1, you must maintain a high level of precision. In science, **The Butterfly Effect** describes how a tiny change in initial conditions can lead to vast differences in the outcome. In weather forecasting, a single decimal point error can mean the difference between predicting a sunny day and a hurricane.

The same is true for your numerical profile. If you get your birth date wrong, or if you make a mistake in your addition, your framework will be skewed. You will be looking at a map for a different life. This is why we insist on using the official records. We want the data to be as "clean" as possible.

Before you begin the calculations in Chapter 1, take a moment to find your birth certificate. Ensure you have the correct year. Many people are surprised to find that the family story of their birth does not match the legal record. In numerology, the legal record is the data point that counts. It is the moment you were officially registered into the collective human framework.

Addressing the Psychological Need for Order

Humans have a deep psychological need for order. This is known as **Closure Need**. According to psychologist **Arie Kruglanski**, people with a high need for closure prefer clear answers and dislike ambiguity. Uncertainty causes stress and anxiety.

Numerical frameworks provide this closure. They take the messy, confusing experience of being human and organize it into nine categories. This provides a sense of relief. When you can say "I am a 4, and that is why I value stability," you are providing yourself with a logical answer to a complex question. This reduces stress and allows you to focus on growth.

However, we must use this order as a tool, not a cage. A framework is meant to support you, not limit you. Just because you are a 7 does not mean you can never be a leader. It just means your leadership style will be informed by your need for analysis. You will be a "thinking leader" rather than a "feeling leader."

The Structure of the Life Path Framework

The Life Path framework is divided into three sections:

1. **The Foundation:** This is your primary Life Path number. It is the core of your framework.
2. **The Master Numbers:** These are the numbers 11, 22, and 33. They represent "advanced" versions of the single digits. They add a layer of complexity to the framework.
3. **The Challenges:** These are the negative or "shadow" traits associated with your number. Every framework has weak points. By identifying them, you can reinforce them.

In this Book, we will cover all three sections. We will start with the basic calculations and then move into the deeper analysis. You will see how these three parts work together to create a complete picture of your life's trajectory.

Why Logic is Your Best Tool

In a world filled with "self-help" advice, it is easy to get lost. Most advice is based on what worked for the person giving it. But you are not that person. You have a different birth date and a different numerical framework. What worked for them might not work for you.

This is why logic is your best tool. By using a repeatable, mathematical system, you are taking the guesswork out of self-improvement. You are using a system that has been tested for thousands of years. You are using the same logic that drives science, music, and architecture.

As you proceed through Book 1, treat the information as raw data. Do not get emotional about the results. If the numbers suggest you are better suited for a path you haven't considered, ask yourself why. Look for the patterns in your past that support the data. You will find that the numbers are often more accurate than your memory.

Preparing for the Work Ahead

You are about to engage in a process of self-discovery that is grounded in facts. This is not about wishing for a better life; it is about calculating a better life. You will need to be diligent with your math and honest with your self-reflection.

The chapters that follow will guide you through each step of the process. We will begin with the calculation of your Life Path number. We will then analyze the traits of each number and look at how they apply to your career and your daily choices. By the end of this Book, you will have a complete map of your life path.

Is it possible to change your path? You cannot change your birth date. You cannot change the framework. But you can change how you move within it. You can choose to walk your path with confidence, or you can struggle against it. This workbook is here to help you choose confidence.

Final Thoughts on Numerical Frameworks

The world is a complex place. Numbers provide the simplicity we need to navigate it. By defining the framework of numerical influence, you are taking the first step toward a more organized and successful life. You are moving from a state of reacting to a state of planning.

Take your time with each section. The work you do here will form the foundation for everything else in this book. Once you understand your framework, the rest of the profile will fall into place. It is time to move from theory to action. Let us begin the calculation.

Summary of the Framework:

- **Birth Date as Anchor:** Your birth date is the primary data point for your life.

- **Temporal Landmarks:** Birthdays serve as psychological fresh starts and baseline data.

- **Resonance and Entrainment:** We are all influenced by the numerical frequency of our birth timing.

- **Pythagorean Qualitative Logic:** Numbers have character and traits, not just quantities.

- **Path vs. Personality:** Your path is your destination; your personality is how you travel.

- **Cycles and Biology:** Life moves in predictable mathematical patterns that match biological growth.

Chapter 1: Calculate Your Life Path Number with Accuracy

The Life Path number is the single most important data point in your numerical profile. In the architecture of your life, if the Overall Introduction provided the blueprints, the Life Path is the foundation upon which the entire structure is built. It is a permanent, immutable marker of your natural tendencies. While your name can change through marriage, professional branding, or personal preference, your birth date is an unalterable fact of history.

This chapter is designed to move you beyond "pop-psychology" numerology and into the realm of **Quantitative Self-Assessment**. We will use the Pythagorean method of reduction to distill your complex birth data into a single, functional frequency.

I. The Mathematical Logic of Temporal Placement

Why do we treat a birth date as data? In the field of **Chronobiology**, researchers study how timing affects biological systems. Everything from the migration of birds to the release of cortisol in the human brain is governed by timing. Your birth date represents your "initial conditions." In **Chaos Theory**, the "Sensitivity to Initial Conditions" (often called the Butterfly Effect) suggests that small differences at the start of a system can lead to vastly different outcomes.

When you calculate your Life Path, you are identifying the specific "initial conditions" of your life. This is not a mystical process; it is a way of categorizing the temporal window through which you entered the world. We use the **Gregorian Calendar**, which is a solar dating system. It is a mathematical model designed to keep human time in sync with the Earth's revolutions around the sun.

The Physics of the "Fresh Start"

In a 2014 study titled *The Fresh Start Effect*, researchers at the University of Pennsylvania found that people are more likely to pursue goals when they perceive a "temporal landmark." Your birth date is the ultimate temporal landmark. It is the 0,0 coordinate on your life's graph. By calculating the number associated with this date, you are defining the "slope" of your life's trajectory.

II. The Three-Part Reduction Method: Structural Integrity

In many casual books on numbers, you might be told to simply add up all the digits of your birth date in a single string. However, for a workbook grounded in logic and precision, we utilize the **Three-Part Reduction Method.** This method preserves the structural integrity of the three distinct cycles that make up your birth: the Month, the Day, and the Year.

1. The Month: The Social Framework

The month of your birth represents the broader seasonal and social influence you were born into. In sociology, this is known as the "cohort effect." People born in the same month often share certain environmental stimuli. Mathematically, the month provides the first "vibration" of the set.

2. The Day: The Individual Identity

The day of your birth is the most "personal" part of the data. While millions share your birth month and year, fewer share the specific day. In physics, this is akin to a "local variable." It defines your core personality and how you interact with the immediate world.

3. The Year: The Generational Cycle

The year represents the long-term historical and ancestral trends. It is the "macro-data." Just as an individual born in 1940 enters a different economic and social framework than someone born in 2000, the year provides the "historical frequency" of your Life Path.

III. Mathematical Proof:
The Digital Root and Casting Out Nines

To understand why we reduce numbers, we must look at **Number Theory**. The process of reducing a number to a single digit is formally known as finding its **Digital Root.**

The Formula for Digital Roots

In formal mathematics, the digital root dr(n) of a number *n* can be expressed using the formula:

dr(n) = 1 + ((n - 1) mod 9)

This formula proves that our reduction system is a valid mathematical operation, not a random game. When you reduce your birth date, you are finding the remainder of your life's total value when divided by the universal cycle of nine.

Why Nine?

The number nine is unique in our base-10 system. Any number multiplied by nine results in digits that add up to nine (e.g., $9 \times 5 = 45$; $4 + 5 = 9$). Nine is the "limit" of our single-digit system. In geometry, a circle has 360 degrees ($3 + 6 + 0 = 9$). In biology, human gestation lasts roughly nine months. The number nine represents the completion of a cycle. By finding your digital root, you are finding your position within that universal cycle of completion.

IV. Step-by-Step Calculation: A Technical Manual

Precision is the difference between a useful map and a dangerous one. Follow these instructions exactly. Use a pen and paper—do not perform this mentally.

Step 1: The Month Reduction

Write your birth month as a number.

- **January to September:** 1 through 9.
- **October:** 10 (1 + 0 = 1)
- **November:** 11 (1 + 1 = 2)
- **December:** 12 (1 + 2 = 3)

Critical Note: In this initial calculation, we reduce November (11) to 2. While 11 is a "Master Number," we are currently looking for your **Base Path.** We will address the "intensity" of Master Numbers in Chapter 3.

Step 2: The Day Reduction

Write the day of your birth. If it is 10 or higher, add the digits together.

- **Example (28th):** 2 + 8 = 10. Then 1 + 0 = 1.
- **Example (11th):** 1 + 1 = 2.
- **Example (22nd):** 2 + 2 = 4.

Step 3: The Year Reduction

This is the "heavy lifting" of the calculation. Add all four digits of your year together.

- **Example (1995):** 1 + 9 + 9 + 5 = 24.
- **Second reduction:** 2 + 4 = 6.
- **Year Result:** 6.

Step 4: The Final Integration

Now, take the three results and add them.

- **Month Result + Day Result + Year Result = Final Sum**
- If the Final Sum is 10 or higher, reduce it one last time (unless it is 11, 22, or 33, which you should circle but still reduce to see the base frequency).

V. Case Studies in Numerical Precision

To validate this logic, let us look at three distinct profiles.

Profile A: The Visionary (1)

Date: October 5, 1985

- **Month:** 10 (1+0=1)
- **Day:** 5
- **Year:** 1985 (1+9+8+5=23 → 5)
- **Final:** 1 + 5 + 5 = 11
- **Base Life Path:** 2 (with an 11 Master frequency).
- **Analysis:** This individual has a base of cooperation (2) but carries the intense visionary drive of the 11.

Profile B: The Architect of Stability (4)

Date: March 21, 1970

- **Month:** 3
- **Day:** 21 (2+1=3)
- **Year:** 1970 (1+9+7+0=17 → 8)
- **Final:** 3 + 3 + 8 = 14 → 5
- **Base Life Path:** 5.
- **Analysis:** Despite a "stable" appearance, the 5 Life Path indicates a core frequency of change and exploration.

VI. The Psychological Impact of "Numerical Anchoring"

In behavioral economics, **Anchoring** is a cognitive bias where an individual relies too heavily on an initial piece of information (the "anchor") when making decisions. Your Life Path serves as a "Positive Anchor."

When you know your number, you have a baseline for your behavior. For example, if you know you are a Life Path 7 (The Analyst), and you are feeling overwhelmed by a loud social event, you can anchor yourself in the data. You aren't "antisocial"; you are simply operating within a frequency that requires more processing time and quiet. This reduces the cortisol response associated with "social shame" and allows for logical self-regulation.

VII. Common Data Entry Errors and Their Consequences

In programming, there is a concept called **GIGO (Garbage In, Garbage Out)**. If the input data is flawed, the output is useless.

1. **The "Linear" Mistake:** Adding 1+0+5+1+9+8+5 in a straight line. While this often yields the same result, it can fail to identify "Master Number" gateways.

2. **The "Legal vs. Biological" Conflict:** Always use the date on your official birth certificate. This is the date you were "registered" into the social system. Numerology, like law, operates on the recorded data of your existence.

3. **The "Zero" Misconception:** In reduction, a 0 is a placeholder. A 10 reduces to 1. The zero "magnifies" the 1 but does not change its core frequency.

VIII. The Biological Rhythm: Circadian vs. Numerical

In medicine, a **Chronotype** is the manifestation of circadian rhythms in an individual.

- **Larks** are productive in the morning.
- **Owls** are productive at night.

Your Life Path is a **Macro-Chronotype**.

- **Paths 1, 2, 3:** The "Morning" of life. High energy, new ideas, initiation.
- **Paths 4, 5, 6:** The "Midday" of life. Management, social interaction, physical labor.
- **Paths 7, 8, 9:** The "Evening" of life. Mastery, completion, introspection, legacy.

If you are a Life Path 8 (a "legacy" path) but you are obsessed with "initiation" (trying to act like a 1), you will experience **Mathematical Friction**. This leads to burnout. This workbook helps you identify your Macro-Chronotype so you can work *with* your timing, not against it.

IX. Practical Workbook: The Reduction Lab

This is the most critical part of Book 1. Perform your calculation three times to ensure there are no errors.

Test 1: The Three-Part Method

1. Month: ____
2. Day: ____
3. Year: ____
4. **Sum:** ____

   Life Path: ____

Test 2: The Modular Check

Take your birth year. Divide it by 9. What is the remainder?

(Example: 1995 / 9 = 221, Remainder 6).

Does this remainder match your Year Reduction from

Test 1?   (Yes/No)

Test 3: The Linear Check

Add every single digit of your birth date together in a row.

__ + __ + __ + __ + __ + __ + __ + __ = ______

Reduce this to a single digit.

Result: ____

Do all three tests produce the same Life Path? If not, re-read the "Step-by-Step" section. Precision is non-negotiable.

X. Conclusion: The Power of the Known

By the end of this chapter, you are no longer a person with a "vague sense of purpose." You are a person with a **numerical coordinate**. You have identified your base frequency.

In **Chapter 2**, we will move from the "What" (the number) to the "How" (the traits). We will explore the nine primary frequencies in exhaustive detail, allowing you to match your observed behavior to the mathematical data.

Chapter 2: Identify the Traits of Single-Digit Numbers One through Nine

Having calculated your Life Path number in Chapter 1, you now possess the raw data of your existence. However, data without interpretation is merely noise. In the same way that a chemist must understand the properties of an element—its boiling point, its reactivity, and its atomic weight—you must understand the qualitative properties of your Life Path number.

This chapter provides a comprehensive, data-driven analysis of the nine primary frequencies that govern human character. To meet the necessary depth of this study, we will examine each number through the lens of **behavioral probability**, **social dynamics**, and **cognitive architecture**.

The Theory of Numerical Archetypes

In psychology, an archetype is a universal, inborn model of a person, personality, or behavior. **Carl Jung** proposed that these archetypes reside in the collective unconscious. In the Pythagorean framework, these archetypes are mapped to the numbers 1 through 9. Each number represents a specific stage in the cycle of development, from the initial spark of creation (1) to the final stage of universal completion (9).

When we analyze these traits, we are looking at **Probability Distributions**. While a Life Path 1 is *more likely* to exhibit leadership traits, environmental factors (upbringing, education, and culture) act as variables that shape how that leadership is expressed.

We will examine each number through four distinct lenses:

1. **The Core Frequency:** The fundamental "why" behind the behavior.

2. **The Behavioral Patterns:** How this number typically interacts with the world.

3. **The Shadow Traits:** The mathematical "inverse" or the negative manifestations of the energy.

4. **The Logical Objective:** The specific "problem" this number is designed to solve.

Life Path 1: The Monad of Innovation and Autonomy

The Number 1 is the mathematical beginning. It is the only number that cannot be divided by anything other than itself. In geometry, it is the point. In biology, it is the single cell.

The Core Frequency

The 1 frequency is driven by **Primary Initiation**. Individuals with this path are hardwired for independence. They are the "pioneers" of the numerical scale. Their internal logic is centered on the self as the primary mover of reality. They operate best when they have a clear, singular goal.

Behavioral Patterns

- **Self-Reliance:** 1s prefer to work alone because it removes the friction of consensus. They value efficiency over social harmony.

- **Decisiveness:** They process information quickly and move toward action without the need for external validation.

- **Innovation:** They are often the first to try a new method or explore a new territory. They are comfortable with the risk of being first.

The Shadow Traits

The shadow of the 1 is **Isolation and Aggression**. When a 1 is out of alignment, their independence becomes "egoism." They may struggle to follow instructions, seeing any form of authority as a personal threat. This can lead to the "lonely at the top" syndrome, where the individual has achieved success but has burned all social bridges in the process.

The Logical Objective

To develop the "Self." The 1 is here to learn that true leadership is not about dominance, but about the courage to stand alone in the pursuit of a vision.

Life Path 2: The Dyad of Cooperation and Synthesis

The Number 2 is the first step toward relationship. It represents the line connecting two points. It is the number of duality: light and dark, action and reaction.

The Core Frequency

The 2 frequency is driven by **Equilibrium**. If the 1 is the "ego," the 2 is the "social contract." These individuals are the "diplomats" of the numerical scale. Their logic is built on the understanding that two forces working together are more powerful than one working in isolation.

Behavioral Patterns

- **Mediation:** 2s have a natural ability to see both sides of an argument. They are the "glue" that holds teams together.
- **Sensitivity:** They are highly attuned to the "emotional data" in a room. They notice what isn't being said.
- **Support:** They often find success by being the "power behind the throne," providing the infrastructure that allows others to shine.

The Shadow Traits

The shadow of the 2 is **Passivity and Over-Sensitivity**. A 2 in shadow may become a "people pleaser," sacrificing their own needs to maintain a false sense of harmony. They can become indecisive, paralyzed by the fear of causing conflict or making the "wrong" choice for the group.

The Logical Objective

To develop "Relatability." The 2 is here to learn that true peace comes from internal balance, not just the absence of external noise.

Life Path 3: The Triad of Expression and Expansion

The Number 3 is the result of 1 and 2 coming together. It represents the triangle, the most stable shape in engineering. It is the number of the "creative spark."

The Core Frequency

The 3 frequency is driven by **Communication**. These individuals are the "messengers." Their internal logic is based on the dissemination of ideas. They are here to take the raw concepts of the 1 and the partnerships of the 2 and turn them into something visible to the public.

Behavioral Patterns

- **Articulacy:** 3s are naturally gifted with words, whether through speaking, writing, or performance.

- **Social Magnetism:** They possess a "vibration" that draws people toward them. They are often the life of the party or the center of a social circle.

- **Optimism:** They see the potential for growth where others see stagnation. They are the "cheerleaders" of the numerical scale.

The Shadow Traits

The shadow of the 3 is **Superficiality and Scattering**. Because they have so many ideas, 3s can struggle with follow-through. They may use their words to manipulate or gossip, wasting their creative energy on "small talk" rather than meaningful expression. They can become "jacks of all trades, masters of none."

The Logical Objective

To develop "Authentic Expression." The 3 is here to learn that words have weight and that their creativity should be used to uplift, not just to entertain.

Life Path 4: The Tetrad of Structure and Practicality

The Number 4 represents the square and the cube. It is the foundation of the physical world (the four seasons, the four elements, the four cardinal directions).

The Core Frequency

The 4 frequency is driven by **Stability**. These individuals are the "builders." Their logic is strictly grounded in the material plane. They value what can be measured, touched, and proven. They are the architects of reality.

Behavioral Patterns

- **Methodology:** 4s do not take shortcuts. They believe that the process is as important as the result.

- **Reliability:** They are the "rocks" of their families and organizations. If a 4 says they will do something, it gets done.

- **Organization:** They have a natural talent for creating systems and managing resources. They thrive in environments with clear rules and boundaries.

The Shadow Traits

The shadow of the 4 is **Rigidity and Dogmatism.** A 4 in shadow can become "stuck in the mud," refusing to adapt to new information because it doesn't fit their established system. They can become workaholics, valuing productivity over human connection and becoming intolerant of those who lack their discipline.

The Logical Objective

To develop "Manifestation." The 4 is here to learn that while structure is necessary, it must be flexible enough to allow for organic growth.

Life Path 5: The Pentad of Freedom and Versatility

The Number 5 is the midpoint of the 1–9 scale. It represents the five senses and the five fingers. It is the number of sensory experience and movement.

The Core Frequency

The 5 frequency is driven by **Adaptability.** These individuals are the "explorers." Their internal logic is centered on the pursuit of freedom. They view life as a series of data-gathering missions and sensory experiments.

Behavioral Patterns

- **Curiosity:** 5s are constantly seeking new experiences, flavors, and ideas. They are the most traveled of all the numbers.

- **Multi-tasking:** They can handle several projects at once, thriving in fast-paced or high-pressure environments.

- **Communication:** Like 3s, they are good with people, but their focus is on the *exchange* of information across cultures and boundaries.

The Shadow Traits

The shadow of the 5 is **Indulgence and Irresponsibility.** A 5 out of balance can become addicted to the "new," abandoning projects and relationships as soon as the initial excitement fades. They may struggle with discipline, seeing any commitment or routine as a cage.

The Logical Objective

To develop "Disciplined Freedom." The 5 is here to learn that true freedom is found through self-mastery and focus, not just the absence of boundaries.

Life Path 6: The Hexad of Responsibility and Nurturing

The Number 6 is often called the "Mother/Father" number. In geometry, it is the hexagon, the most efficient shape for packing (as seen in honeycombs).

The Core Frequency

The 6 frequency is driven by **Harmonization**. These individuals are the "caregivers." Their logic is based on the home, the family, and the community. They feel a mathematical pull toward correcting imbalances in their immediate environment.

Behavioral Patterns

- **Responsibility:** 6s naturally step up when a job needs to be done, especially if it involves taking care of others or maintaining a group.

- **Aesthetics:** They have a keen eye for beauty and strive to make their surroundings comfortable and artistic. They are the designers of the numbers.

- **Empathy:** They are the "counselors" of the numerical scale, providing a safe space for others to heal and grow.

The Shadow Traits

The shadow of the 6 is **Intrusiveness and Martyrdom**. A 6 in shadow can become "The Meddler," trying to fix people who do not want to be fixed. They may take on too much responsibility and then resent others for not appreciating their sacrifice, leading to "emotional burnout."

The Logical Objective

To develop "Service without Attachment." The 6 is here to learn that they can love and care for others without taking ownership of their problems or requiring a specific outcome.

Life Path 7: The Heptad of Analysis and Introspection

The Number 7 is the "seeker." It is the number of the seven days of the week and the seven colors of the rainbow. It represents the bridge between the material and the analytical.

The Core Frequency

The 7 frequency is driven by **Investigation**. These individuals are the "analysts." Their internal logic is centered on finding the "truth" behind the surface level of reality. They are the researchers and scientists.

Behavioral Patterns

- **Intellectualism:** 7s spend a great deal of time in their own heads, processing data and observing patterns. They value depth over breadth.

- **Solitude:** They require regular periods of isolation to "recharge" their mental batteries. They are often private and introverted.

- **Skepticism:** They have a built-in "nonsense detector" and question everything until they find empirical or logical proof.

The Shadow Traits

The shadow of the 7 is **Aloofness and Paranoia**. A 7 in shadow can become cold and detached, hiding their emotions behind a wall of logic. They may become overly suspicious of others' motives, leading to extreme social isolation and a cynical worldview.

The Logical Objective

To develop "Faith in Knowledge." The 7 is here to learn that not everything can be solved with the mind—some truths must be experienced through intuition and connection.

Life Path 8: The Ogdoad of Power and Manifestation

The Number 8 is the symbol of infinity turned on its side. It represents the flow of energy: "As above, so below." It is the number of material success and karmic balance.

The Core Frequency

The 8 frequency is driven by **Authority**. These individuals are the "executives." Their logic is built on the accumulation of power and resources to achieve large-scale goals. They understand the mechanics of the world.

Behavioral Patterns

- **Ambition:** 8s have a natural drive to be at the top of their chosen field. They are motivated by status, legacy, and results.
- **Efficiency:** They have an instinct for business, finance, and the management of large systems. They see the "big picture" of resource management.
- **Resilience:** They are built to handle high-pressure situations and recover quickly from financial or professional setbacks.

The Shadow Traits

The shadow of the 8 is **Greed and Ruthlessness**. An 8 out of balance can become obsessed with money and status, stepping on others to reach the top. They may struggle with a "power trip," using their authority to dominate rather than to lead, often leading to their own eventual downfall.

The Logical Objective

To develop "Ethical Abundance." The 8 is here to learn that true power is a tool for the greater good, not an end in itself.

Life Path 9: The Ennead of Compassion and Completion

The Number 9 is the final single digit. It contains all the numbers that come before it. It is the number of the "humanitarian" and the global citizen.

The Core Frequency

The 9 frequency is driven by **Universalism**. These individuals are the "philosophers." Their logic is focused on the big picture and the collective. They are less concerned with individual gain and more concerned with the evolution of society.

Behavioral Patterns

- **Tolerance:** 9s are often very open-minded, seeing the common thread in all cultures and religions. They are the most progressive of the numbers.
- **Generosity:** They give freely of their time, money, and energy to causes they believe in.
- **Completion:** They are often brought into situations to "close the door" or finish what others have started. They represent the "end of the cycle."

The Shadow Traits

The shadow of the 9 is **Emotional Drama and Disillusionment**. A 9 in shadow can become overwhelmed by the suffering of the world, leading to a "savior complex" or deep bitterness when people do not follow their altruistic advice. They may struggle to let go of the past.

The Logical Objective

To develop "Selfless Wisdom." The 9 is here to learn that by letting go of personal ego, they can become a vessel for universal truth and healing.

The Quantitative Analysis of Character Interactions

While knowing your number is the first step, understanding how these frequencies interact is the key to mastering your Life Path. In physics, waves can undergo **Constructive Interference** (where they build each other up) or **Destructive Interference** (where they cancel each other out).

For example, a Life Path 1 (pioneer) and a Life Path 4 (builder) can create a powerful team. The 1 provides the vision, and the 4 provides the infrastructure. This is constructive interference. However, if they are not aware of their traits, the 1 may see the 4 as "too slow," and the 4 may see the 1 as "too reckless." This is destructive interference.

Statistical Normalization of Your Traits

It is vital to remember that no one is 100% their Life Path number. In statistics, we use the **Normal Distribution** (or Bell Curve). Most people fall into the middle of the curve for their number. You might possess 70% of the traits of a 5, while the other 30% are influenced by your name (Book 2) and your current cycle (Book 3).

Workbook: Match Your Traits to Your Primary Number

This workbook section is designed to move the information from Chapter 2 out of the realm of theory and into the realm of **Applied Data**. To gain value from this framework, you must perform a "Historical Audit" of your own behavior. By mapping your past actions against the qualitative traits of your Life Path, you verify the accuracy of the system and identify areas where you are currently operating in the "Shadow" frequency.

Part 1: The Alignment Audit

In this section, you will analyze three major life events through the lens of your Life Path number.

Event 1: A Significant Success

Describe a time when you felt completely in "flow"—a moment where you succeeded with minimal friction.

- **The Event:** ____
- **The Numerical Connection:** Look at the traits of your Life Path in Chapter 2. Which specific trait was active during this success? (e.g., if you are a 4, was it your *methodology* or *organization*?)
- **Trait:** ____
  ____

Event 2: A Significant Conflict

Describe a time when you felt "blocked" or experienced recurring friction with others.

- **The Event:** ____
- **The Numerical Connection:** Which "Shadow Trait" of your number was likely triggered during this conflict? (e.g., if you are an 8, was it *ruthlessness*? If you are a 2, was it *passivity*?)
- **Shadow Trait:** ____
  ____

Event 3: A Major Transition

Describe a time you chose to change your path (career, relationship, or location).

- **The Event:** ____
- **The Numerical Connection:** How did your "Core Frequency" drive this change? (e.g., a 5 changing for *freedom*, or a 6 changing for *responsibility*).
- **Core Driver:** ____
  ____

Part 2: The Qualitative Trait Checklist

Review the detailed list for your specific Life Path in Chapter 2. Rate yourself on a scale of 1 to 10 (1 = low expression, 10 = high expression) for each of the primary behavioral patterns.

Your Life Path Number: ______

Trait / Behavioral Pattern	Rating (1-10)	Evidence from your life
Pattern A: (e.g., 1's Self-Reliance)		
Pattern B: (e.g., 1's Innovation)		
Pattern C: (e.g., 1's Decisiveness)		
Shadow X: (e.g., 1's Aggression)		

Part 3: Identifying the "Frequency Gap"

In electrical engineering, a **Phase Shift** occurs when two waves are out of alignment. If your current life feels difficult, you may be experiencing a "Life Phase Shift."

Compare your **Current Daily Activities** to your **Logical Objective** found in Chapter 2.

1. **Current Daily Output:** What do you spend 80% of your time doing?

    ____

    ____

    ____

    ____

2. **Your Numerical Objective:** (e.g., 7 is "To develop Faith in Knowledge")

    ____

    ____

    ____

    ____

3. **The Gap:** Is your daily output serving your objective? (Low / Medium / High)

    ____

    ____

    ____

    ____

Part 4: Logical Correction Plan

Using the data from Parts 1-3, write one specific logical correction you can make this week to align more closely with your core frequency.

- **Logic:** "Because my Life Path is _____________________________, I am naturally built for _______________________________ ."

- **Observation:** "Currently, I am wasting energy on ____________ (Shadow Trait/Misaligned Activity)."

- **Correction:** "I will reallocate 2 hours this week toward _______ (Core Behavioral Pattern)."

Chapter 3: Manage the Intensity of Master Numbers Eleven, Twenty-Two, and Thirty-Three

In the analysis of any complex data set, we occasionally encounter "anomalies"—points of data that possess significantly higher values than the standard deviation allows. In the Pythagorean framework, the numbers 1 through 9 represent the standard spectrum of human experience. However, the numbers 11, 22, and 33 act as **scalar quantities** with added magnitude. These are known as the **Master Numbers**.

If the single-digit Life Paths act as the standard residential power grid (110V/220V) designed to fuel a stable, productive life, the Master Numbers act as high-voltage transmission lines (110kV+). They carry a double charge of frequency. While this potential allows for massive output, it also comes with inherent risks. Without a proper "step-down transformer" (psychological maturity and physical grounding), this high voltage can fry the system, leading to burnout, anxiety, and existential paralysis.

This chapter is a technical manual for those who carry these numbers. It is designed to move you from a state of being overwhelmed by your potential to a state of managing your "voltage" with precision.

I. The Physics of the "Standing Wave"

To understand why Master Numbers are different, we must look at the physics of wave interference. In acoustics and wave theory, when two waves of the same frequency meet, they create **Constructive Interference**. This results in a wave with the same frequency but double the amplitude (height/power).

- **11** is the constructive interference of two 1s.
- **22** is the constructive interference of two 2s.
- **33** is the constructive interference of two 3s.

This creates a phenomenon known as a **Standing Wave**. For the individual, this manifests as a constant, internal resonance that does not dissipate. While a Life Path 1 finishes a task and rests, a Master Number 11 feels a continuous "hum" of potential energy that demands expression.

II. The Law of Delayed Maturity

One of the most critical concepts in understanding Master Numbers is the **Law of Delayed Maturity**. In developmental psychology, we know that the human prefrontal cortex—the area responsible for executive function and long-term planning—does not fully mature until the mid-20s.

For Master Numbers, the "spiritual maturity" required to handle their frequency often does not arrive until the mid-30s or 40s.

- **The Early Years (0–30):** Most Master Numbers operate primarily as their "reduced" single digit during this time. An 11 lives as a 2; a 22 lives as a 4. If they try to access the full Master power too early, they often experience "short circuits" in the form of nervous breakdowns or lack of direction.

- **The Integration Phase (35+):** As the individual gains life experience, they gradually learn to integrate the high-frequency energy without destabilizing their life.

If you are a young Master Number feeling lost, understand that you are essentially a jet engine mounted on a bicycle. You are currently building the "fuselage" (life experience) necessary to handle your engine.

III. Master Number 11: The Illuminator

Equation: $1 + 1 = 2$ (with High-Voltage Potential)

Archetype: The Psychic Antenna / The Visionary

Correlate: High Sensory Processing Sensitivity (SPS)

The 11 is the most intuitive of all numbers. It combines the fierce independence and leadership of the 1 with the extreme sensitivity and collaboration of the 2. This creates a dynamic tension: the drive to stand out (1) versus the drive to blend in and harmonize (2).

The Cognitive Architecture of the 11

The brain of an 11 functions like a high-gain antenna. In psychological terms, 11s often score very high on the **HSP (Highly Sensitive Person)** scale. They process sensory data—tone of voice, micro-expressions, atmospheric shifts—that others filter out.

- **The Superpower:** "Instant Knowing." The 11 does not always need linear logic to reach a conclusion. They can leap from A to Z via intuition. They are the visionaries who see trends before they exist.

- **The Voltage Risk:** Nervous Tension. Because the antenna never turns off, 11s are prone to anxiety, insomnia, and nervous exhaustion. They are often misdiagnosed with attention disorders because their brains are processing too much background data.

The Shadow Frequency

When an 11 cannot ground their energy, they become **The Fanatic**. They may escape into illusion, conspiracy theories, or spiritual bypassing to avoid the harshness of the real world. They become "idea generators" who never manifest anything, trapped in the loop of potential.

The Management Protocol

The 11 requires **Grounding**. They must translate their abstract intuition into concrete logic. If an 11 has a "vision," they must force themselves to write a business plan (the work of the 4) or build a team (the work of the 2).

IV. Master Number 22: The Master Builder

Equation: $2 + 2 = 4$ (with High-Voltage Potential)

Archetype: The Architect / The Industrialist

Correlate: Systems Thinking & Structural Engineering

The 22 is often called the "Power Number." It combines the intuitive, relational diplomacy of the 2 with the grounded, disciplined structural logic of the 4. This is a rare combination. Usually, people are either "dreamers" (right brain) or "doers" (left brain). The 22 is both.

The Cognitive Architecture of the 22

The 22 possesses a mind built for **Systems Theory**. They naturally understand how complex parts fit together to form a whole. Whether it is international supply chains, architectural blueprints, or organizational hierarchies, the 22 sees the "skeleton" of the system.

- **The Superpower:** Scalable Manifestation. A 4 builds a house; a 22 plans a city. They have the ability to execute massive projects that affect thousands of people. They bridge the gap between the "impossible" and the "practical."

- **The Voltage Risk:** The Burden of Potential. 22s often suffer from a crippling fear of failure because their internal standard is so high. If they are not changing the world, they feel like failures. This can lead to "paralysis by analysis," where the 22 achieves nothing because they are waiting for the "perfect" opportunity.

The Shadow Frequency

When a 22 goes dark, they become **The Exploiter**. They may use their understanding of systems to manipulate others for personal gain. Alternatively, they become the "Drudgery Worker," a 22 who has rejected their power and lives a small, frustrated life as a limited 4, constantly feeling that they have missed their destiny.

The Management Protocol

The 22 requires **Incremental Scale**. They must learn to trust that small foundations support large structures. A 22 must not despise "small beginnings." They must engage in physical building—gardening, construction, coding—to keep their high mental energy rooted in physical reality.

V. Master Number 33: The Master Teacher

Equation: $3 + 3 = 6$ (with High-Voltage Potential)

Archetype: The Avatar / The Healer

Correlate: Hyper-Empathy & Mirror Neurons

The 33 is the rarest and most spiritually demanding of the numbers. It combines the expressive, joyful communication of the 3 with the nurturing, self-sacrificing service of the 6. It is a frequency of "Universal Love."

The Cognitive Architecture of the 33

The 33 appears to have highly active **Mirror Neurons**—the brain cells that allow us to feel what others are feeling. The 33 does not just sympathize; they literally "feel" the collective emotion of their environment.

- **The Superpower:** Transcendent Communication. The 33 has the ability to speak or create art that heals. When they speak, they bypass the intellect and speak directly to the emotional center of the audience. They are the great teachers, spiritual leaders, and healers who sacrifice their lives for a cause.

- **The Voltage Risk:** Total Burnout. The 33 often lacks boundaries. They are the "Cosmic Martyrs." They give until they physically collapse. They can be crushed by the weight of the world's suffering because they lack the filter to shut it out.

The Shadow Frequency

When a 33 is out of alignment, they become **The Meddlesome Martyr.** They help where help is not wanted, creating dependency in others to validate their own worth. They may become emotionally volatile, swinging between extreme benevolence and deep, depressive withdrawal.

The Management Protocol

The 33 requires **detached compassion.** They must learn the difference between "supporting" and "carrying." Their lesson is that they cannot save everyone, and that their first responsibility is to the stability of their own vessel (the body).

VI. The "Hidden" Master Numbers (44, 55, etc.)

You may ask, "What about 44 or 55?" In the Pythagorean system, we generally stop analyzing character at 33. This is because numbers beyond 33 represent frequencies that are largely incompatible with ordinary human life.

- **44 (The Master Disciplinarian):** Often associated with military generals or massive structural overhauls.

- **55 (The Master Catalyst):** Associated with revolutionary, explosive change.

While these numbers exist mathematically, they operate on a transpersonal level. For the purpose of this personal profile, we focus on 11, 22, and 33 as the primary agents of human evolution.

VII. Managing the Electrical Load: Practical Strategies

If you have a Master Number, you cannot live like a standard number. You require a different maintenance schedule for your mind and body.

1. The Nervous System Reset (Vagus Nerve Stimulation)

Master Numbers (especially 11s and 33s) have overactive sympathetic nervous systems (fight or flight). You must manually engage the parasympathetic system.

- **Protocol:** Cold water immersion (face or body) for 30 seconds daily. This stimulates the Vagus nerve and forces the high-voltage energy to ground.

2. The Creative Discharge

Energy that is not expressed turns into anxiety. You must have a "useless" creative outlet.

- **Protocol:** Master Numbers must engage in art, building, or writing *without the intent to sell it*. This acts as a pressure valve, allowing the Master energy to flow without the pressure of the "Material" world.

3. The "Container" Concept

Master energy is like water; without a container, it spills everywhere. You need a container (a routine).

- **Protocol:** Strict adherence to circadian rhythms. Sleep and wake at the same time. Eat at the same time. The predictability of the routine (The 4 energy) provides a safe container for the chaotic inspiration of the Master Number.

VIII. Conclusion: The Burden and the Blessing

Possessing a Master Number is not a ticket to an easy life; it is a contract for a demanding one. You have been given a double portion of energy because you have a double portion of work to do.

Do not envy the Life Path 5 who can travel freely, or the Life Path 3 who can play lightly. You are here for heavy lifting. You are the structural engineers (22), the illuminators (11), and the healers (33) of the human race. When you accept this responsibility and learn to manage your internal voltage, the friction disappears, and you become a force of nature.

Workbook: Evaluate the Influence of Double Digits in Your Profile

This workbook section is critical for anyone with an 11, 22, or 33 in their chart (Life Path, Month, Day, or Year). If you are a single digit (e.g., Life Path 1), check if you have Master Numbers in your sub-cycles (e.g., born in November, the 11th month).

Part 1: The Voltage Diagnostic

We need to determine if you are currently handling your voltage or if you are "short-circuiting." Rate the following symptoms of "Master Number Misalignment" on a scale of 0 (Never) to 5 (Constant).

The 11 Symptoms (Nervous Tension):

1. I have trouble shutting off my brain at night.   (__)
2. I feel an inexplicable sense of urgency, like I'm running out of time.   (__)
3. I get sudden flashes of insight that I cannot explain logically.   (__)

The 22 Symptoms (Structural Pressure):

1. I feel a crushing sense of responsibility to do something "huge."   (__)
2. I am frustrated by the incompetence or slowness of systems around me.   (__)

3. I oscillate between feeling powerful and feeling completely
   paralyzed. (__)

The 33 Symptoms (Emotional Overload):

1. I physically feel the pain or stress of the people in the room
   with me. (__)
2. I often sacrifice my own health or finances to help others. (__)
3. People treat me like a "confessional," telling me their
   deepest secrets. (__)

Total Score: _______ / 45

- **0-15:** Low Voltage / Dormant Phase.
- **16-30:** Active Phase / Moderate Friction.
- **31-45:** Critical Overload. Immediate grounding required.

Part 2: The "Bridge" Exercise

The challenge of the Master Number is bridging the "Vision" with the "Reality." You must identify your **Base** (the reduced number) and your **Master** (the double number).

My Profile:

- **My Master Number:** (e.g., 22) _______________________________
- **My Base Number:** (e.g., 4) _______________________________

The Gap Analysis:

1. **The Master Vision:** What is the "impossible" thing I dream of doing? (e.g., "Ending hunger in my city," "Building a global company.")

   ____

   ____

   ____

   ____

2. **The Base Reality:** What is the small, boring, practical step I am avoiding? (e.g., "Balancing my checkbook," "Volunteering at a soup kitchen once a week.")

   ____

   ____

   ____

   ____

3. **The Integration:** I will use the **Base Reality** to serve the **Master Vision** by doing this specific task tomorrow:

Part 3: The Shadow Audit

Master Numbers cast long shadows. Be honest about which "Shadow Archetype" you fall into when you are stressed.

- **11 Shadow:** The Fanatic / The Neurotic. (Do you spiral into anxiety?)

- **22 Shadow:** The Tyrant / The Drudge. (Do you control others or give up completely?)

- **33 Shadow:** The Martyr / The Meddler. (Do you save people who didn't ask to be saved?)

My Primary Shadow: _______________________________________

My Trigger: I tend to fall into this shadow when... (e.g., "I am tired," "I am criticized.")

Part 4: The Grounding Contract

To manage this energy, you must commit to a physical protocol. Choose one from the list below or create your own based on the "Management Protocols" in the chapter.

- [ ] **Earthing:** 10 minutes of barefoot contact with grass/soil daily.

- [ ] **Heavy Lifting:** 3x weekly resistance training to exhaust nervous energy.

- [ ] **Silence:** 15 minutes of absolute silence (no input) daily.

- [ ] **Water:** Cold shower finish (30 seconds) daily.

Signed Commitment: _______________________________________

Chapter 4: Align Your Professional Career with Your Birth Path

Work is not merely a method of economic survival; it is the primary venue where you expend your life force energy. In physics, work is defined as force applied over a distance. In your life, your career is the "distance" you travel, and your Life Path number determines the specific type of "force" you are designed to apply.

When your career aligns with your numerical frequency, you experience **Flow**—a psychological state defined by Mihaly Csikszentmihalyi as complete immersion and energized focus. When your career opposes your frequency, you experience **Friction**. In mechanical engineering, friction creates heat and wear. In human beings, this friction manifests as burnout, resentment, and chronic fatigue.

This chapter is a strategic audit of your professional life. We will move beyond vague career advice and use your data to determine exactly where you fit in the global economy. We will identify the specific roles, environments, and operational modes that maximize your output while minimizing your metabolic cost.

I. The Thermodynamics of Professional Success

Why do some people work 80 hours a week and feel energized, while others work 40 hours and feel destroyed? The answer lies in the **Thermodynamics of Personality**.

Every Life Path operates on a specific fuel source and emits a specific type of output.

- **Input:** What stimulates you (Interaction, Solitude, Risk, Safety).

- **Output:** What you produce (Ideas, Objects, Systems, Feelings).

If you are a Life Path 4 (The Builder) working in a chaotic, high-risk sales environment (a Life Path 5 domain), you are burning energy just to *exist* in that space, before you even do any work. Your system is fighting the environment. This is inefficient.

By aligning your career with your Life Path, you achieve **Energetic Efficiency**. You stop fighting your nature and start leveraging it. This is the secret to high performance. It is not about working harder; it is about working with the grain of your own wood.

II. The Concept of "Numerical Competence"

We often choose careers based on what we are *taught* to do, not what we are *designed* to do. We must distinguish between **Learned Competence** and **Numerical Competence**.

- **Learned Competence:** Skills you have acquired through schooling or necessity. You *can* do it, but it drains you.

- **Numerical Competence:** Skills that are innate to your frequency. You do them naturally, often without realizing they are skills.

This chapter classifies the nine Life Paths into **Professional Archetypes**. As you read, look for your Natural Competence, not just your current job title.

III. The Professional Archetypes (1–9)

Life Path 1: The Independent Operator

Archetype: The Entrepreneur / The Specialist / The CEO

Core Driver: Autonomy

The 1 is biologically wired for self-direction. In a corporate hierarchy, a 1 creates friction if they are placed in middle management where they must constantly seek permission.

- **Ideal Environment:** Startups, consultancy, freelance work, or high-level leadership where the "chain of command" is short.

- **The Trap:** Being a "Cog." If a 1 is micromanaged, they become toxic or depressed. They need ownership of their results.

- **Pivot Strategy:** If you are stuck in a corporate job, seek a role with "intrapreneurial" freedom—a project where you are the sole lead.

Life Path 2: The Diplomatic Facilitator

Archetype: The Mediator / The HR Specialist / The Strategic Partner

Core Driver: Collaboration

The 2 thrives in the "space between" people. They are the oil in the engine. They are not designed for isolation.

- **Ideal Environment:** Human resources, counseling, account management, diplomacy, nursing. Any role where success is defined by relationship maintenance.

- **The Trap:** High-Conflict Sales. A 2 in a "cut-throat" competitive environment will suffer nervous system overload. They need cooperation, not combat.

- **Pivot Strategy:** Move away from quota-based solo work and toward client success or team management roles.

Life Path 3: The Creative Communicator

Archetype: The Marketer / The Performer / The Spokesperson

Core Driver: Expression

The 3 is the "Voice." Their value in the economy is their ability to persuade, entertain, and inform.

- **Ideal Environment:** Sales (relationship-based), marketing, PR, acting, writing, teaching. Any role where words are the primary tool.

- **The Trap:** The Silent Office. A 3 in a data-entry job or a silent laboratory will wither. They need social feedback loops to regulate their energy.

- **Pivot Strategy:** If you are in a technical field, pivot to the *communication* side of that field (e.g., Technical Sales, Training).

Life Path 4: The Structural Architect

Archetype: The Engineer / The Accountant / The Project Manager

Core Driver: Stability and Order

The 4 provides the foundation. They are the immune system of a company, identifying risks and ensuring protocols are followed.

- **Ideal Environment:** Banking, law, construction, engineering, logistics. Any role where precision and methodology are valued over speed or improvisation.

- **The Trap:** The Chaos Startup. A 4 in a disorganized, "move fast and break things" environment will experience extreme anxiety. They need rules and predictable outcomes.

- **Pivot Strategy:** Seek industries that are regulated and established. Move from "Idea Generation" to "Operations."

Life Path 5: The Dynamic Catalyst

Archetype: The Promoter / The Traveler / The Consultant

Core Driver: Variety and Freedom

The 5 is the agent of change. They are designed to circulate information and products. They are the blood flow of the economy.

- **Ideal Environment:** Travel industry, investigative journalism, event planning, outside sales. Any role where no two days are the same.

- **The Trap:** The Cubicle. A 5 in a 9-to-5 desk job with a strict routine is a ticking time bomb. They will eventually self-sabotage just to create excitement.

- **Pivot Strategy:** Negotiate for remote work, travel opportunities, or project-based work that allows for sprints of intensity followed by rest.

Life Path 6: The Responsible Guardian

Archetype: The Educator / The Healer / The Designer

Core Driver: Harmony and Service

The 6 brings function and beauty together. They are the "nesters" of the workplace, often taking on the emotional labor of the team.

- **Ideal Environment:** Healthcare, education, interior design, non-profit management, customer service. Any role that improves the quality of life for others.

- **The Trap:** The Soulless Corp. A 6 working for a company with unethical practices or a toxic culture will become deeply cynical. They need to believe in the product.

- **Pivot Strategy:** Align your skills with a mission-driven organization. If you are in finance, move to ethical investing.

Life Path 7: The Analytical Specialist

Archetype: The Scientist / The Researcher / The Strategist

Core Driver: Knowledge and Truth

The 7 is the "Brain." They are paid for what they know and what they can solve, not how many hands they shake.

- **Ideal Environment:** Academia, data science, specialized medicine, IT, detective work. Roles that require deep work and solitude.

- **The Trap:** The Open-Plan Office. A 7 forced to endure constant noise and interruptions cannot function. They need a door that closes.

- **Pivot Strategy:** Specialize. Become the "go-to" expert in a niche field that allows you to work autonomously.

Life Path 8: The Executive Director

Archetype: The CFO / The Business Owner / The Administrator

Core Driver: Power and Result

The 8 is the "Will." They understand value, money, and hierarchy. They are designed to bear the weight of decision-making.

- **Ideal Environment:** Finance, corporate management, real estate, law, military command. Any role where the stakes are high and the rewards are tangible.

- **The Trap:** The Subordinate Role. An 8 with no authority is a caged lion. They will inevitably clash with incompetent leadership.

- **Pivot Strategy:** If you cannot own the company, ensure you own your department. Negotiate for profit-sharing or performance-based pay.

Life Path 9: The Global Humanitarian

Archetype: The Philanthropist / The Creative Visionary / The Diplomat

Core Driver: Impact

The 9 is the "Soul." They see the big picture and are driven by how their work affects the collective.

- **Ideal Environment:** International relations, environmental science, arts, social work, holistic health. Roles that bridge cultures or heal communities.

- **The Trap:** The Profit-Only Grind. A 9 working solely to make a shareholder rich will feel a deep sense of emptiness. They need a "Why."

- **Pivot Strategy:** Look for the Corporate Social Responsibility (CSR) wing of your industry, or move into the non-profit or creative sector.

IV. Master Numbers in the Workforce

If you possess a Master Number (11, 22, 33), your career path is often non-linear. You are likely to bloom later in life.

- **The 11 Career:** You are a "Lightning Rod." You belong in roles that require intuition and inspiration—spiritual leadership, visionary tech, or inspirational speaking. You are not a worker bee; you are the Queen Bee's advisor.

- **The 22 Career:** You are a "Empire Builder." You need massive scale. You are suited for international architecture, global logistics, or government planning. Small businesses will feel suffocating.

- **The 33 Career:** You are a "Cosmic Parent." You belong in high-level mentorship. You might lead a hospital, a movement, or a school. You must lead with the heart.

V. The Phenomenon of "Numerical Dissonance"

Numerical Dissonance occurs when your job requires you to use a frequency that is the "Shadow" of your Life Path.

- *Example:* A Life Path 1 (Independence) working as a Personal Assistant (Service/Subordination).

- *Result:* The 1 becomes resentful and arrogant. They may be fired for "attitude problems," but the real problem is energetic misalignment.
- *Example:* A Life Path 7 (Privacy/Analysis) working in Retail Sales (Constant Interaction).
- *Result:* The 7 experiences "social hangover" every day. They become cold and robotic to customers as a defense mechanism.

Burnout is rarely about the *volume* of work. It is about the *type* of work. A Life Path 4 can do 12 hours of spreadsheets and feel fine. A Life Path 3 would be suicidal after 4 hours of the same task.

VI. The Strategic Pivot: Evolution, Not Revolution

If you realize you are in the wrong career, do not panic. Do not quit tomorrow. Numerology teaches **Cycles**. We must transition intelligently.

1. **The Intra-Role Shift:** Can you change *how* you do your current job? If you are a 5 (Variety) stuck in a 4 (Routine) job, can you ask to be the person who travels to different branches?
2. **The Lateral Move:** Can you move to a different department? If you are a 2 (People) in the Finance Dept (Numbers), can you move to HR (People)?
3. **The Side Hustle:** Test your Life Path frequency on the weekends. If you are an 8 trapped in a low-level job, start a small business on the side to feed your need for authority.

VII. Conclusion: Your Career as a Vehicle

Your career is not you. It is the vehicle you drive. If you are trying to drive a tractor (Life Path 4 energy) on a Formula 1 track (Life Path 5 environment), you will crash.

By understanding the mechanics of your vehicle, you can choose the right track. When you do this, work ceases to be a struggle and becomes a form of self-actualization. You are paid to be yourself.

Workbook: Inventory Your Natural Skills and Work Preferences

This workbook uses the **"Skill-Frequency Match"** technique to audit your current professional life and plan your future trajectory.

Part 1: The "Flow" Audit

Review your work history. Identify tasks, not job titles.

1. **The "Time-Warp" Task:** What is one work task where time seems to disappear? (e.g., "Designing slides," "Negotiating deals," "Organizing files").

   ____

   ____

   ____

2. **The "Drain" Task:** What is one task that you procrastinate on because it drains you instantly?

   ____

   ____

   ____

3. **Numerical Check:** Look at your Life Path traits in Chapter 2.
   - Does the "Time-Warp" task align with your Core Frequency? (Yes/No)
   - Does the "Drain" task align with your Shadow or a conflicting number? (Yes/No)

Part 2: Environmental Assessment

Rate your current work environment against your Needs.

My Life Path Number: _______

My Critical Needs (Refer to Section III):

- Need 1: (e.g., Autonomy) _______________________________
- Need 2: (e.g., Silence) _______________________________

Current Job Rating (1-10):

- How well does my job meet Need 1? _______________________
- How well does my job meet Need 2? _______________________

Total "Fit" Score: _______ / 20. (If below 12, a pivot plan is required).

Part 3: The Pivot Strategy

If you need to change, define the "Next Step" using the **Evolution vs. Revolution** model.

- **Option A (Evolution):** What is one conversation I can have with my current boss to align my role better with my number? (e.g., "Ask to lead a project," "Ask for a quiet workspace.")

  ____

  ____

  ____

- **Option B (Revolution):** If I had to leave, what is one job title that perfectly matches my Archetype?

  ____

  ____

  ____

Part 4: The Skill Translation

Write down your top 3 "Hard Skills" (e.g., Coding, Writing, Sales). Now, translate them into your Life Path language.

- *Example:* Skill: Coding.
    - *If Life Path 4:* "Building stable infrastructure."
    - *If Life Path 1:* "Creating a new app startup."
    - *If Life Path 7:* "Analyzing data patterns."

My Skill Translation:

1. Skill: _________ → Life Path Application: _______________
2. Skill: _________ → Life Path Application: _______________

Conclusion: You do not need to throw away your resume. You simply need to reframe your skills to serve your natural frequency.

Chapter 5: Apply Your Life Path Knowledge to Daily Decision Making

You have calculated your core frequency (Chapter 1), identified your psychological traits (Chapter 2), managed your intensity (Chapter 3), and aligned your career (Chapter 4). Now, we arrive at the granular level of existence: **The Micro-Decision.**

It is estimated that the average adult makes over 35,000 remotely conscious decisions per day. From what to eat for breakfast to how to respond to a stressful email, these micro-decisions act as the individual pixels that form the high-resolution image of your life.

Most people suffer from **Decision Fatigue.** In psychology, this is the deteriorating quality of decisions made by an individual after a long session of decision making. This happens because most people treat every choice as a new variable.

In this chapter, we will turn your Life Path number into a **Filtering Algorithm.** Instead of analyzing every choice from scratch, you will run your options through the logic gate of your specific frequency. This reduces cognitive load, minimizes regret, and ensures that your daily life remains in phase with your macro-trajectory.

I. The Physics of Choice: Entropy vs. Alignment

In thermodynamics, **Entropy** is a measure of disorder. In your life, entropy increases when you make choices that are dissonant with your core frequency.

- **Dissonant Choice:** A Life Path 1 (Autonomy) choosing to attend a three-hour committee meeting where they have no voting power.
  - *Result:* High friction, energy loss, irritability.
- **Resonant Choice:** A Life Path 1 declining the meeting to work on a solo project.
  - *Result:* Low friction, energy gain, "Flow."

Your goal is to automate as many decisions as possible by pre-setting your criteria based on your number. This is not about being rigid; it is about being **aerodynamic**.

II. The Decision Matrix by Number

Below are the specific **Decision Protocols** for each Life Path. These protocols act as your "Standard Operating Procedure" (SOP) for daily choices.

Life Path 1: The Commander Protocol

- **The Driver:** Speed and Autonomy.
- **The Pitfall:** Impulsiveness. 1s decide so fast they often skip critical details.
- **The Protocol:** "The 10% Delay."
  - Because you are wired for speed, you must artificially insert a delay. When faced with a decision, make your choice instantly in your head, but **wait 10% of the timeline** before announcing it. This allows your brain to catch any glaring errors without stifling your decisiveness.
- **The Binary Filter:** "Does this allow me to lead, or does it force me to follow?"

Life Path 2: The Consensus Protocol

- **The Driver:** Harmony and Connection.
- **The Pitfall:** The "Yes" Trap. 2s often agree to things they don't want to do to avoid awkwardness.

- **The Protocol:** "The Default Pause."
  - o Never say "Yes" in the room. Your nervous system is too attuned to the other person's emotions. Adopt the phrase: *"Let me check my capacity and get back to you."* This separates you from the emotional pressure and allows you to decide logically.
- **The Binary Filter:** "Is this reciprocal? Will I receive as much support as I am giving?"

Life Path 3: The Expressive Protocol

- **The Driver:** Joy and Creativity.
- **The Pitfall:** The "Shiny Object" Syndrome. 3s say yes to everything that sounds fun in the moment, leading to a calendar full of obligations they later resent.
- **The Protocol:** "The Energy Audit."
  - o Visualize doing the task *next Tuesday.* Do you feel heavy or light? The 3 has a somatic (body-based) truth detector. If the thought of doing it later feels heavy, the answer is no.
- **The Binary Filter:** "Does this allow me to express my authentic self, or am I performing for others?"

Life Path 4: The Architect Protocol

- **The Driver:** Security and Order.
- **The Pitfall:** Analysis Paralysis. 4s want 100% of the data before acting. Since 100% data is impossible, they often stall.
- **The Protocol:** "The 80% Rule."
  - o Once you have 80% of the information, you must execute. The final 20% of certainty comes from doing the work, not thinking about it. Trust your foundation.
- **The Binary Filter:** "Is this a sustainable risk? Does this build upon my existing foundation?"

Life Path 5: The Explorer Protocol

- **The Driver:** Freedom and Sensory Input.
- **The Pitfall:** Escapism. 5s often choose the option that offers the quickest exit or the biggest thrill, ignoring long-term consequences.

- **The Protocol:** "The Cage Check."
  - o Before saying yes, ask: "How hard is it to get out of this?" 5s need exit strategies. If a decision binds you for 5 years without a break clause, your nervous system will eventually revolt. Build flexibility into your commitments.
- **The Binary Filter:** "Does this expand my world or contract it?"

Life Path 6: The Guardian Protocol

- **The Driver:** Responsibility and Care.
- **The Pitfall:** Over-Functioning. 6s decide to "fix" things that aren't broken or aren't their business.
- **The Protocol:** "The Lane Check."
  - o Ask yourself: *"Is this my lane?"* If you are fixing a problem for a competent adult, you are stealing their lesson. Your decision should focus on your immediate sphere of responsibility (home/family/team), not the whole world.
- **The Binary Filter:** "Am I doing this out of love, or out of obligation/guilt?"

Life Path 7: The Analyst Protocol

- **The Driver:** Truth and Privacy.
- **The Pitfall:** Over-Intellectualization. 7s can debate the pros and cons until the opportunity passes. They also despise being rushed.
- **The Protocol:** "The Solitude Seal."
  - o **Never decide in a meeting.** The 7 brain requires silence to process data. Establish a rule: "I do not make decisions while people are talking to me." Retreat, process, then return with the answer.
- **The Binary Filter:** "Do I have enough data? Is this logically sound?"

Life Path 8: The Executive Protocol

- **The Driver:** ROI (Return on Investment) and Efficiency.
- **The Pitfall:** Domination. 8s can make decisions that are good for the bottom line but disastrous for human morale.
- **The Protocol:** "The Human Impact Assessment."

o You are already good at the math. Before executing, force yourself to look at the *people* cost. A decision that makes money but loses the team is a bad decision.

- **The Binary Filter:** "Does this increase my long-term value and authority?"

Life Path 9: The Humanitarian Protocol

- **The Driver:** Impact and Integrity.

- **The Pitfall:** Emotional Burnout. 9s often decide based on what will "save" the most people, ignoring their own resources.

- **The Protocol:** "The Integrity Scan."

    o Does this align with your highest principles? A 9 cannot work for a paycheck alone. If the decision violates your ethics, no amount of logic can make it work.

- **The Binary Filter:** "Does this serve the greater good without destroying my personal well-being?"

III. The Master Number "Pause" (11, 22, 33)

If you carry a Master Number, your decision-making process is more complex because you are processing on two channels simultaneously (The Base and The Master).

The 24-Hour Rule: Master Numbers should almost **never** make significant decisions on the same day.

- **Channel 1 (The Base):** Your logical brain might say "Yes" to a job because it pays well (4).

- **Channel 2 (The Master):** Your intuitive brain might scream "No" because it senses the company is ethically corrupt (22).

It takes time for these two signals to integrate. Sleep is the integration mechanism. If you decide in the moment, you usually listen to the Base and regret ignoring the Master. **Sleep on it. The correct answer will be there in the morning.**

IV. Conflict Resolution: The "Phase Match"

Conflict usually arises when two people are trying to resolve a problem using different numerical protocols.

- **Scenario:** A Life Path 1 (Fast/Decisive) is arguing with a Life Path 7 (Slow/Analytical) about buying a house.

- **The Friction:** The 1 wants to put in an offer *now*. The 7 wants to research the flood plain history for three days. The 1 thinks the 7 is stalling; the 7 thinks the 1 is reckless.

- **The Solution:** Recognize the frequency.
  - The 1 must say: *"I respect your need for data. How much time do you need?"*
  - The 7 must say: *"I respect your need for action. I will have the answer by Friday at noon."*

By naming the frequency, you depersonalize the conflict. You aren't fighting each other; you are negotiating between two different operating systems.

V. Managing "Decision Fatigue" with Numerology

To conserve your mental energy for the big decisions, you must automate the small ones based on your number. This is called **Architecting Your Default State**.

- **For the 4 (Order):** Automate your wardrobe and meal plan. Eliminate chaos from the morning routine.

- **For the 5 (Variety):** Automate your "Foundation" (bills, savings) so you can be spontaneous with your free time without guilt.

- **For the 2 (Connection):** Automate your social calendar. Set recurring dates so you don't have to constantly negotiate times.

VI. Conclusion: The Compound Effect

A single micro-decision seems irrelevant. But over ten years, the difference between a Life Path 7 who takes time to think (Protocol) and a Life Path 7 who lets others rush them (Shadow) is the difference between a genius and a recluse.

You are now equipped with the logic to navigate your daily existence. You have the blueprint (Chap 1), the traits (Chap 2), the power management (Chap 3), the career map (Chap 4), and the daily compass (Chap 5).

You are ready to graduate from this introductory workbook.

Workbook: The Micro-Decision Laboratory

This section is designed to stress-test your decision-making protocols. You will track your choices for 3 days to identify where you are leaking energy.

Part 1: The Decision Autopsy

Think of a "bad" decision you made recently. Dissect it.

1. **The Decision:** ____

2. **The Pressure:** Why did you make it? (e.g., "I felt rushed," "I felt guilty," "I wanted to impress.")

____

____

____

3. **The Numerical Error:** Look at your Protocol in Section II. What rule did you break? (e.g., A 2 who didn't use the "Default Pause.")

____

____

____

Part 2: The Scripting Exercise

You must have scripts ready for when the world tries to push you off your number. Write your **"No" Script** based on your Life Path.

- *Example (Life Path 5):* "That sounds like a great commitment, but I need to keep my schedule flexible right now, so I have to decline."

- *Example (Life Path 6):* "I would love to help, but I have to focus on my own family obligations this week."

- *Example (Life Path 7):* "I need some time to process this information. I cannot give you an answer in this meeting."

My Custom Script:

____

____

____

____

____

Part 3: The 3-Day Challenge

For the next 72 hours, apply your **Specific Protocol** (from Section II) to *every* decision that requires more than 5 minutes of your time.

Day 1 Check-in:

- Did I use the protocol? (Yes/No)
- Did I feel more or less drained? (More/Less)

Day 2 Check-in:

- Did I use the protocol? (Yes/No)
- Did I feel more or less drained? (More/Less)

Day 3 Check-in:

- Did I use the protocol? (Yes/No)
- Did I feel more or less drained? (More/Less)

Conclusion: Summarize the Impact of Your Primary Number

We have reached the terminal phase of **Book 1: The Blueprint**. Throughout this journey, we have navigated the transition from raw, chronological data to a complex, multidimensional understanding of your life's energetic architecture. By this stage, the concept of a "Life Path number" should have evolved in your mind. It is no longer a static label or a casual descriptor; it is a **functional frequency**—the baseline vibration upon which every experience, relationship, and achievement in your life is constructed.

To conclude this volume, we must engage in a deep-dive synthesis. This conclusion serves as your technical summary, exploring the long-term impact of numerical alignment on your biology, your psychology, and your legacy. We will examine the macro-consequences of living "in phase" versus "out of phase" with your primary frequency.

I. The Thermodynamics of the Self: Efficiency vs. Entropy

In physics, the Second Law of Thermodynamics states that the total entropy of an isolated system can never decrease over time; it can only remain constant or increase. In human terms, **Entropy** manifests as disorder, fatigue, and the gradual breakdown of our physical and mental systems.

When you live in opposition to your Life Path number, you are increasing your internal entropy. Every hour spent in a career that clashes with your frequency, or every relationship maintained through the suppression of your core traits, acts as a "leak" in your system.

The Metabolic Cost of Dissonance

If you are a Life Path 4 (The Builder) forced into a Life Path 5 (The Catalyst) role—constantly improvising, traveling, and lacking structure—your brain must expend a significant amount of glucose and oxygen just to suppress your natural urge for order. This is **Metabolic Friction**. Over a decade, this friction leads to:

- **Systemic Inflammation:** Chronic stress caused by misalignment triggers the body's fight-or-flight response.

- **Cognitive Decline:** The "prefrontal drain" of acting against your nature reduces your ability to make high-level decisions.

- **Identity Erosion:** Eventually, you lose track of where the "mask" ends and the "self" begins.

Conversely, **Alignment** creates a state of **Negentropy** (negative entropy). When a Life Path 7 (The Analyst) spends their day in deep, quiet research, their environment matches their internal frequency. This creates a feedback loop of energy. The work doesn't drain them; it fuels them.

II. The Impact on Biological Rhythms and Health

Data suggests that individuals who live in alignment with their core archetypes report higher levels of subjective well-being and lower incidences of stress-related illnesses. Your Life Path number dictates your "Ideal Operating Rhythm."

- **Numbers 1, 5, and 8 (High Intensity):** These frequencies require high-output periods followed by complete "power downs." Their impact is felt in the adrenal system. Misalignment for these numbers often leads to burnout or cardiovascular tension.

- **Numbers 2, 6, and 9 (Social/Cyclical):** These frequencies thrive on rhythmic, relational consistency. Their impact is felt in the hormonal system (oxytocin and serotonin). Misalignment leads to a sense of profound isolation or "emotional anemia."

- **Numbers 3, 4, and 7 (Mental/Structural):** These frequencies require cognitive clarity. Their impact is felt in the nervous system. Misalignment leads to sensory overload, anxiety, and sleep disorders.

By summarizing the impact of your number, we recognize that it is a **Health Protocol.** Living your number is the most basic form of preventative medicine.

III. The Psychological Impact: The Integration of the Shadow

Throughout Chapter 2, we discussed the "Shadow Traits" of each number. A major impact of mastering Book 1 is the **transmutation of the Shadow.**

When you do not understand your number, your Shadow traits (like the 1's aggression or the 6's meddling) feel like personality flaws that you must hide. This creates a "split" in the psyche. However, when you view these through the lens of numerical data, you realize the Shadow is simply **misdirected frequency.**

The 1's aggression is actually misplaced leadership. The 8's greed is actually misplaced manifestation power. The impact of this realization is profound: you stop judging yourself and start **calibrating** yourself. This leads to **Radical Self-Acceptance**, which is the psychological foundation for all future growth.

IV. The Social Impact: Your Frequency as a Service

We often think of our Life Path as a private journey. However, the impact of your number is most visible in your "Social Contribution." Every number represents a specific "Resource" in the human ecosystem.

- **The 1 provides the Spark.**
- **The 2 provides the Glue.**
- **The 3 provides the Voice.**
- **The 4 provides the Foundation.**

- **The 5 provides the Change.**
- **The 6 provides the Care.**
- **The 7 provides the Truth.**
- **The 8 provides the Means.**
- **The 9 provides the Vision.**

When you do not live your number, the ecosystem suffers. If you are a 4 but you are trying to be a 5, the world loses a solid foundation and gains a mediocre catalyst. The impact of your alignment is that you finally fill the specific "hole" in the world that only your frequency can plug.

V. Summarizing the Professional and Decisional Legacy

In Chapters 4 and 5, we explored career and daily choices. The cumulative impact here is your **Legacy**.

A legacy is not just what you leave in a will; it is the "Vibrational Trace" you leave in the lives of others. An 8 who has mastered their frequency leaves a legacy of empowered systems and ethical abundance. A 3 who has mastered their frequency leaves a legacy of inspired ideas and lifted spirits.

By using your **Binary Filters** and **Decision Protocols**, you ensure that your legacy is intentional. You stop being a "reaction" to your environment and start being an "action" upon it.

VI. Conclusion: The Transition to the Social Mask

Book 1 has given you the **Internal Blueprint**. You now know how the engine works. You know the fuel it needs, the speed it can handle, and the maintenance it requires.

However, an engine is useless if it is not connected to a chassis and wheels. In the Pythagorean system, your Life Path is your "Soul's Intent," but your **Name**—which we will calculate in Book 2—is your **Social Interface**. It is how you show up in the world.

Sometimes, your Name and your Life Path are in a state of **Harmonic Resonance** (they help each other). Other times, they are in a state of **Dissonance** (they challenge each other). For example, you might have the soul of a 7 (Seeker of Solitude) but a name that vibrates to a 3 (Social Performer). This creates a specific "mask" that can either hide your true self or provide a bridge to help you share your wisdom.

Before we move to Book 2, you must finalize your relationship with your Blueprint through the following workbook exercises.

Workbook: Final Alignment Audit and Integration

This final workbook section for Book 1 is designed to turn the words of theory in this chapter into a concrete "Operating Manual" for your life.

Part 1: The "Dissonance" Inventory

We must identify the exact points where you are currently losing energy.

1. **The Role Dissonance:** List one area of your life where you are acting like a number that is NOT yours. (e.g., "At my job, I have to act like a 4, but I am a 5.")

    ____

    ____

    ____

2. **The Shadow Cost:** What is the specific price you pay for this dissonance? (e.g., "I feel angry every Sunday night," "I have constant headaches.")

    ____

    ____

    ____

3. **The Tactical Pivot:** Based on Chapter 4, what is one "Micro-Adjustment" you can make to move this role 10% closer to your actual frequency?

    ____

    ____

    ____

Part 2: The "Mastery" Manifesto

Create a one-sentence "Identity Statement" that synthesizes the data from all 5 chapters.

"I am a Life Path **[Number]**, built for **[Core Driver]**, designed to work as a **[Archetype]**, and I protect my energy by using the **[Decision Protocol]**."

Part 3: The Frequency Maintenance Schedule

To maintain the impact of your number, you must have a "Maintenance Schedule." Based on your number's needs, define your daily, weekly, and monthly requirements.

Interval	Requirement (Based on your number's needs)
Daily	(e.g., 20 mins of silence for a 7, or a high-intensity workout for an 8)
Weekly	(e.g., A creative project for a 3, or a family dinner for a 6)
Monthly	(e.g., A trip to a new place for a 5, or a budget review for a 4)

Part 4: Additional Questions

1. What is the single most important "Data Point" you learned about yourself in Book 1?

    ____

    ____

    ____

2. In what specific way has your "Decision Fatigue" decreased since applying your numerical filters?

    ____

    ____

    ____

3. Are you ready to stop being a "Generalist" and start being a "Specialist" in your own frequency? What is the first thing you need to let go of to make that happen?

    ____

    ____

    ____

Reflection Questions: Assess Your Connection to Your Life Path

You have reached the final technical requirement of **Book 1: The Blueprint.** While the previous chapters have provided the raw data, the archetypes, and the logical protocols, this chapter is designed for **Deep Integration.** In the field of cognitive science, information only becomes "knowledge" when it is synthesized through the lens of personal experience.

The following reflection module is not a casual survey; it is a **Socratic Audit.** These questions are engineered to bypass your "Social Mask" and speak directly to your "Numerical Core." By answering these extensively, you will bridge the gap between merely knowing your number and actively *living* your frequency.

I. The Historical Audit: Retroactive Alignment

To understand where you are going, we must perform a forensic analysis of where you have been. Your life has likely left a trail of "numerical breadcrumbs" long before you ever learned the mathematics behind them.

1. The Childhood Impulse

Before the world told you who you should be, how did you naturally spend your time?

- **For 1s and 8s:** Were you the one organizing the game or playing solo with a specific goal?
- **For 2s and 6s:** Were you the peacemaker among friends or the one "nurturing" your toys?
- **For 7s and 4s:** Were you the one taking things apart to see how they worked or lost in a book?

Reflection: Describe your favorite childhood activity. How did that activity express your core frequency?

2. The Crisis Response

When everything falls apart, we regress to our primary frequency. Think of the most stressful event of your last five years. Did you isolate (7), take command (1/8), seek comfort in others (2/6), or try to build a logical plan out of the chaos (4)?

Reflection: Analyze your behavior during this crisis. In what ways did your Life Path "Shadow" emerge, and in what ways did your Life Path "Strength" provide the solution?

II. The Biological and Energetic Audit

Your body is the hardware that runs your numerical software. If the hardware is not calibrated to the software, you experience "System Lag."

3. The Somatic Signal

Where do you feel "Resonance" in your body? When you are doing something that perfectly aligns with your number (e.g., a **3** performing or a **5** exploring), what is the physical sensation? Conversely, how does dissonance feel?

Reflection: Map the physical sensations of alignment versus dissonance. Does dissonance manifest as a tight chest, a clouded mind, or chronic fatigue?

4. The Recovery Protocol

Mastering your number means mastering your recovery. High-intensity numbers (**1, 5, 8**) require physical grounding, while sensitive numbers (**2, 7, 11**) require sensory deprivation.

Reflection: Are you currently recovering in a way that actually replenishes your specific frequency, or are you using "generic" relaxation that leaves you feeling more drained?

III. The Professional and Legacy Audit

Your career is the "Work" ($W = F \times d$) of your life—the distance you travel through the application of your natural force.

5. The "Invisible Work" Analysis

In every job, there is "Invisible Work"—the labor you do that isn't in your job description but you do anyway because of your frequency. (e.g., The **6** who mediates office drama, or the **7** who fact-checks every meeting).

Reflection: What is the "invisible work" you find yourself doing regardless of your job title? How does this prove the dominance of your Life Path?

6. The Resource Contribution

If you were the only person of your Life Path number in a room of 100 people, what is the one thing the room would be missing if you left?

Reflection: Define your "Frequency Value." Why is the world objectively more efficient because your specific number is in the mix?

IV. The Shadow and Transmutation Audit

The Shadow is not a "bad" part of you; it is where your greatest potential energy is currently trapped or misdirected.

7. The "Repulsion" Test

What trait in *other* people irritates you the most? Psychological projection suggests we are most repelled by traits we are suppressing in ourselves. (e.g., A **1** might be repelled by "bossy" people because they are suppressing their own leadership).

Reflection: Identify your greatest "Pet Peeve" in others. How does this mirror a Shadow trait of your own number that you haven't yet integrated?

8. The Martyrdom Check

Where are you "Over-Functioning"? (Doing things for others that they should do for themselves). This is a common trap for **2s, 6s, and 9s.**

Reflection: List three things you do out of "Obligation." If you stopped doing them tomorrow, would the world end, or would you simply be forced to sit with the discomfort of your number's true needs?

V. Synthesis: The Path Ahead

9. The "Phase Shift" Correction

If you could change one thing about your current daily environment to make it "Phase Match" your number, what would it be?

Reflection: Write a short "Ideal Day" script from the perspective of your Life Path. What does a day look like where every hour is resonant with your frequency?

Workbook: Deep Reflection Log

Instructions: Spend at least 15 minutes on each of the following prompts to finalize your Book 1 Blueprint.

1. **The Historical Pattern:** Identify a time you felt completely "broken." How did your Shadow frequency contribute to the breakdown, and how did your Core Frequency help you rebuild?

   ____

   ____

   ____

2. **Environmental Ranking:** Rank your current environment (Home, Work, Social) on a scale of 1–10 for "Numerical Compatibility." Which one will you influence first?

   ____

   ____

   ____

3. **The Mastery Commitment:** What is the one logical "Non-Negotiable" you are establishing today to protect your Life Path? (e.g., "I will never accept a job that requires constant interruption.")

   ____

   ____

   ____

BOOK TWO:
Uncover Your Soul's Blueprint

Introduction: Analyze the Inner Drivers of Human Behavior

In Book 1, we calculated your **Life Path,** the immutable "Engine" of your existence derived from your birth date. While that number defines your primary trajectory and the hardware of your life, it does not account for the "Operator" behind the wheel or the specific "Interior Design" of the vehicle. To understand the full complexity of human behavior, we must transition from the external road to the internal architecture. This is the central premise of **Book 2: Uncover Your Soul's Blueprint.**

While your birth date is a fixed cosmic coordinate—a moment in time when the universe whispered a specific frequency—your **Name** is a social, psychological, and linguistic gift. It is the first data set assigned to you by your environment, carrying specific vibrations that shape your internal motivations and your social interface. In the Pythagorean tradition, letters are not merely phonetic markers; they are placeholders for numerical values that, when decoded, reveal the **Inner Drivers** of your personality.

I. The Ontological Weight of a Name: Why Titles Matter

The act of naming is perhaps the most significant human ritual. Across almost every civilization, from the ancient Egyptians who believed the *Ren* (name) was a vital part of the soul, to modern parents spending months deliberating over syllables, we instinctively know that a name is not just a label. It is a **Vibrational Blueprint.**

In linguistics, we often discuss "Nominal Determinism"—the hypothesis that people tend to gravitate toward areas of work that fit their names. In Numerology, we take this a step further. We argue that the specific combination of vowels and consonants in your full legal name at birth creates a persistent resonance. This resonance acts as a filter through which you view the world and, more importantly, through which the world views you.

If the Life Path is the "Plot" of your movie, the Name numbers represent the "Character Development." You can have two people on a Life Path 5 (The Explorer), but if one has a Soul Urge of 4 (Stability) and the other has a Soul Urge of 3 (Expression), their "Exploration" will look entirely different. One will explore through the lens of structural engineering; the other will explore through the lens of investigative journalism.

II. The Triad of Identity: Core, Capacity, and Interface

To analyze human behavior with clinical precision, we utilize a structural triad derived from your full legal name. This framework explains the three layers of the human psyche:

1. The Heart's Desire (Soul Urge): The "Subterranean Motivation"

Calculated from the **vowels** of your name, this number reveals what you crave at the deepest level. Vowels are the "breath" of a name; they carry the emotion and the spirit. The Soul Urge tells us the "Why" behind your ambitions. It is your private truth—the things you want that you might not even tell your closest friends. It is the driver of your emotional satisfaction.

2. The Expression (Destiny): The "Total Potential"

Calculated from the **sum of all letters**, this number represents the "Whole Man." It is the totality of your natural talents, your inherited capabilities, and the "destiny" you are meant to fulfill. If the Life Path is the *direction*, the Expression is the *tool kit* you brought with you to get there.

3. The Personality Number: The "Social Mask"

Calculated from the **consonants**, this number represents the "Front Stage" of your life. Consonants provide the structure and the "shell" of a name. This number is your outward-facing interface—the way people perceive you within the first ten minutes of meeting. It is your protective layer and your marketing department.

III. The Psychology of the "Inner Driver"

Why do we choose the paths we do? Standard behavioral psychology often focuses on external incentives—the "carrots and sticks" of society. However, by analyzing your **Heart's Desire**, we pivot toward **Intrinsic Motivation.**

According to **Self-Determination Theory (SDT)**, humans have three basic psychological needs: autonomy, competence, and relatedness. Your Soul Urge number specifies *how* those needs manifest for you.

- A **Soul Urge 1** finds autonomy through solitary achievement.

- A **Soul Urge 2** finds relatedness through intimate, one-on-one harmony.

- A **Soul Urge 8** finds competence through the accumulation and management of power.

When your Life Path (what you are doing) and your Heart's Desire (what you crave) are in alignment, you experience high psychological resolve. This is what we call **Sovereignty**. However, when they are in conflict, you suffer from **Cognitive Dissonance**.

Case Study: The Reluctant Leader

Imagine an individual with a **Life Path 1** (The Leader) but a **Soul Urge 2** (The Peacemaker). Their external circumstances and natural trajectory constantly push them into the spotlight and into positions of authority. However, their soul craves quiet partnership and the avoidance of conflict. This person will likely be a highly successful but deeply stressed leader, constantly feeling like they are betraying their true nature to fulfill their destiny.

IV. The Social Mask:
Jung, Goffman, and the Personality Number

Human beings are inherently social, requiring a functional "Mask" to navigate the world. In analytical psychology, Carl Jung called this the **Persona**. He argued that the Persona is a necessity for survival—it allows us to interact with others without exposing our raw, vulnerable core in every transaction.

Sociologist **Erving Goffman** took this further in his work on *Dramaturgy*, suggesting that we are all "performing" on a stage. Your **Personality Number** is the script for that performance.

- If you have a **Personality 7**, people will naturally see you as wise, mysterious, or perhaps aloof. They will treat you with a certain intellectual respect.

- If you have a **Personality 3**, people will see you as approachable, fun, and communicative. They will naturally gravitate toward you for social interaction.

The danger lies in **Desynchronization**. If the mask (Personality) is too heavy or too disparate from the internal blueprint (Life Path and Soul Urge), the individual loses their sense of "Self." They begin to believe the performance is the reality. Book 2 provides the diagnostic tools to ensure your mask is a **bridge**, not a **barrier**.

V. The Expression:
Inherited Talents and the "Destiny" Frequency

The **Expression Number** is often called the "Destiny" because it represents the culmination of your name's energy. It is the most "practical" of the name numbers. While the Soul Urge is what you *want* and the Personality is how you *look*, the Expression is what you can actually *do*.

In genetics, we talk about "Gene Expression"—the process by which information from a gene is used in the synthesis of a functional gene product. In Numerology, your Expression Number is the "Functional Product" of your identity. It is the skill set that feels most natural to you.

- An **Expression 4** is naturally gifted at organization and logistics.

- An **Expression 9** is naturally gifted at seeing the "big picture" and handling humanitarian complexities.

By uncovering this blueprint, you stop trying to "learn" skills that are contrary to your frequency and start **refining** the talents you already possess.

VI. The Conflict of Numbers:
Resolving Internal Friction

The most powerful aspect of Book 2 is the analysis of **Numerical Conflict**. Most people feel like a walking contradiction. You might want to be famous (Soul Urge 3) but feel terrified of being judged (Personality 7). You might be a visionary (Life Path 11) but find yourself stuck in the minutiae of accounting (Expression 4).

These are not personality flaws; they are **Data Mismatches**. By mapping these numbers against each other, we can create a "Peace Treaty" within your profile. We learn to use the Expression 4 to build the platform that allows the Life Path 11 vision to reach the world. We learn to use the Personality 7's mystery to add gravitas to the Soul Urge 3's performance.

VII. Emotional Intelligence and the Blueprint

Finally, Book 2 serves as a manual for **Emotional Intelligence (EQ)**. EQ is defined as the ability to perceive, control, and evaluate emotions. Most EQ training is generic. However, a **Personalized EQ** acknowledges that a Life Path 8 processes anger differently than a Life Path 2.

Using your Soul's Blueprint, you will learn to "Strengthen Your Emotional Intelligence" (Chapter 5) by recognizing your specific triggers. You will understand why certain social situations drain you while others energize you, based on the interaction between your Soul Urge and your Personality Mask.

VIII. Technical Methodology:
The Pythagorean Alpha-Numeric Conversion

Before we dive into the calculations, it is vital to understand the "Why" behind the math. We use the **Pythagorean System**, which assigns a number from 1 to 9 to each letter of the Latin alphabet. This is not arbitrary; it is based on the sequence of the letters and their corresponding vibrational "notes."

1	2	3	4	5	6	7	8	9
A	B	C	D	E	F	G	H	I
J	K	L	M	N	O	P	Q	R
S	T	U	V	W	X	Y	Z	

In the coming chapters, we will use this table to dissect your full legal name. We use the legal name given at birth because that is the "Contract" you signed with the physical world upon arrival. Even if you changed your name later, the birth name remains the "Root" of your Expression.

IX. Summary: From Blueprint to Architecture

Book 1 gave you the "Plot." Book 2 gives you the "Character." By synthesizing these two volumes, you move from a two-dimensional understanding of yourself to a three-dimensional, high-resolution model.

You are no longer a victim of your "moods" or your "contradictions." You are a conscious operator of a complex, beautiful, and highly efficient numerical system. It is time to uncover the drivers that make you who you are.

Chapter 1: Compute Your Heart's Desire to Find Internal Motivation

If the **Life Path** (explored in Book 1) is the map of the road you are traveling, the **Heart's Desire**—often referred to in classical numerology as the **Soul Urge**—is the fuel in your tank and the private playlist in your ears. It is the most intimate of all your numbers. While your Life Path describes your external actions and the Expression describes your physical talents, the Heart's Desire describes your **hunger**.

In the Pythagorean system, the Heart's Desire is calculated using exclusively the **vowels** of your full legal name at birth. To understand why, we must look at the intersection of phonetics and metaphysics. Consonants are the "bones" of language; they provide structure, stop the flow of air, and define the shape of a word. Vowels, however, are the "breath." They represent the unobstructed flow of life force. In ancient traditions, the breath was synonymous with the soul— *pneuma* in Greek, *prana* in Sanskrit, or *ruach* in Hebrew. Therefore, the vowels of your name reveal the unobstructed desires of your soul—what you crave when no one is watching and there is nothing to prove to the social world.

I. The Metaphysics of the "Breath" (Vowels)

Vowels represent the internal, emotional, and spiritual aspects of the human experience. In sacred geometry and ancient chanting, it was believed that vowels were the sounds of the planets and the celestial spheres. Because vowels are produced without blocking the breath with the teeth, tongue, or lips, they signify the "pure output" of our internal vibration.

When you speak your own name, the vowels carry the emotional weight. Try it: say your name but remove the consonants. You are left with a series of pure tones. These tones are the frequency of your internal motivation. In this chapter, we are going to isolate those tones to discover the "Why" behind your behavior.

II. The Science of Intrinsic Motivation: Autotelic States

Psychologists categorize motivation into two primary types: **Extrinsic** and **Intrinsic**.

1. **Extrinsic Motivation:** Driven by external rewards—money, status, avoiding punishment, or social validation.

2. **Intrinsic Motivation:** Driven by internal satisfaction—curiosity, the joy of the task itself, or a sense of inherent purpose.

The Heart's Desire is the ultimate diagnostic for your **Intrinsic Drive**.

When you operate from your Heart's Desire, you experience what researchers call **Autotelic Activity** (from the Greek *autos*, "self," and *telos*, "goal"). An autotelic activity is an activity that is an end in itself. You do it because the doing of it nourishes your core frequency.

If you are currently struggling with chronic procrastination, burnout, or a sense of "unearned success," you likely have a **Motivation Mismatch**. You are achieving things that your Life Path is capable of (Extrinsic), but your Soul Urge is being starved (Intrinsic). By computing this number, we identify the exact fuel your soul requires to maintain peak output without the psychological friction of resentment.

III. The Technical Calculation:
Extracting the Soul's Frequency

To compute your Heart's Desire, we use the Pythagorean conversion table. In this specific chapter, we are stripping away the consonants (the "shell") and focusing entirely on the vowels: **A, E, I, O, U.**

1. The Vowel Conversion Table

Vowel	Numerical Value
A	1
E	5
I	9
O	6
U	3

2. The "Y" Rule: The Conditional Vowel

In numerology, the letter **Y** is treated as a vowel *only* when it sounds like a vowel and functions as the only vowel in the syllable.

- **Y is a vowel if:** There are no other vowels in the syllable (e.g., *Lynn, Sky, Bryan, Yolanda*—if the 'Y' creates the 'i' or 'ee' sound).

- **Y is a consonant if:** It is used as a hard 'Y' sound next to another vowel (e.g., *Yesterday, Yellow, Young*).

3. The Formula for Reduction

For those who appreciate the underlying math, the reduction of your name to a single digit follows the principle of the **Digital Root:**

$$f(n) = (n - 1) \bmod 9 + 1$$

However, we calculate each name (First, Middle, Last) separately before combining them, as each name carries its own "vibrational layer" from your lineage and personal identity.

4. Step-by-Step Methodology

1. **Write your full legal birth name** (as it appears on your birth certificate).

2. **Extract the vowels** from each name separately.

3. **Assign values** using the table above.

4. **Sum each name** and reduce it to a single digit (unless it is a Master Number 11, 22, or 33).

5. **Add the results together** for the final Heart's Desire.

> **Example: ANNA MARIE SMITH**
> - **ANNA:** A(1) + A(1) = **2**
> - **MARIE:** A(1) + I(9) + E(5) = 15 → 1 + 5 = **6**
> - **SMITH:** I(9) = **9**
> - **Total:** 2 + 6 + 9 = 17 → 1 + 7 = **8**
> - *Result: Anna has a Heart's Desire of 8.*

IV. The Deep-Dive Meanings: Decoding Your Hidden Hunger

Once you have computed your number, you can analyze your internal "Why." These descriptions focus on the **Subterranean Need**—the hunger that persists even when you are successful.

Heart's Desire 1: The Craving for Individualism

Your soul is nourished by **Autonomy**. You are driven by a subterranean need to be self-sufficient and to prove your own competence. You don't necessarily want to lead others for the sake of power; you want to lead yourself because you cannot stand the inefficiency of following others.

- **The Secret Hunger:** To be "The Only." To do something that has never been done.

- **The Shadow:** Self-absorption. If you don't find a healthy outlet for this individualism, you become a "contrarian" just for the sake of being different.

- **The Decision Filter:** "Does this choice allow me to maintain my independence, or does it make me a cog in someone else's machine?"

Heart's Desire 2: The Craving for Unity

Your soul is nourished by **Harmony and Connection**. You are the "peacemaker" not because you are weak, but because you are highly sensitive to the discord in the environment. You crave partnership, intimacy, and being part of a "we."

- **The Secret Hunger:** To be understood and to create a safe, peaceful "cocoon" for yourself and others.

- **The Shadow:** Codependency. You may sacrifice your own truth just to keep the peace.

- **The Decision Filter:** "Will this foster a deeper connection, or will it create unnecessary friction?"

Heart's Desire 3: The Craving for Self-Expression

Your soul is nourished by **Joy and Communication**. You are the natural "Artist" of life. If you cannot express your inner thoughts, your nervous system begins to fray. You crave social interaction, laughter, and the ability to lift the spirits of others.

- **The Secret Hunger:** To be heard and to be seen in your most authentic, creative state.

- **The Shadow:** Superficiality. You may scatter your energy in a thousand directions, performing for others while feeling empty inside.

- **The Decision Filter:** "Does this allow me to express my truth, or am I suppressing my voice?"

Heart's Desire 4: The Craving for Order

Your soul is nourished by **Structure and Tangibility**. You find peace in a job well done, a clean spreadsheet, or a house built on a solid foundation. You crave the "long game." You are the one who stays the course when everyone else gets distracted.

- **The Secret Hunger:** Security and a legacy that outlasts your own life.

- **The Shadow:** Rigidity. You may become so obsessed with "the rules" that you lose the ability to adapt to a changing world.

- **The Decision Filter:** "Does this build toward a permanent foundation, or is it a fleeting distraction?"

Heart's Desire 5: The Craving for Freedom

Your soul is nourished by **Variety and Sensory Experience**. You are a "sensory seeker." You crave travel, new foods, new people, and the ability to change your mind at a moment's notice. For you, routine is a slow death.

- **The Secret Hunger:** Absolute personal freedom and the removal of all cages.

- **The Shadow:** Escapism. You may run away from commitment the moment things become "boring," missing out on the depth that only comes through time.

- **The Decision Filter:** "Does this expand my world, or does it contract my freedom?"

Heart's Desire 6: The Craving for Responsibility

Your soul is nourished by **Service and the Home**. You are the "Global Nurturer." You find deep satisfaction in taking care of others, creating beauty in your domestic sphere, and being the person everyone relies on in a crisis.

- **The Secret Hunger:** To be needed and to create a "sanctuary" for your loved ones.
- **The Shadow:** Martyrdom. You may take on so much responsibility for others that you become resentful, "smothering" those you intend to help.
- **The Decision Filter:** "Am I acting out of love and responsibility, or out of a need to control the outcome?"

Heart's Desire 7: The Craving for Truth

Your soul is nourished by **Solitude and Wisdom**. You are the "Seeker." You don't want the superficial answer; you want the *correct* one. Your soul requires periods of complete silence and isolation to process the data of the world.

- **The Secret Hunger:** Spiritual or intellectual mastery.
- **The Shadow:** Aloofness. You may become so detached and analytical that you lose the ability to relate to other human beings on an emotional level.
- **The Decision Filter:** "Does this allow for deep analysis and solitude, or is it too noisy and superficial?"

Heart's Desire 8: The Craving for Manifestation

Your soul is nourished by **Power and Material Impact**. You have a subterranean drive to command resources. Whether it's money, authority, or a massive project, your soul wants to see its internal force reflected in the physical world.

- **The Secret Hunger:** Mastery and the ability to influence systems at scale.
- **The Shadow:** Ruthlessness. You may become so obsessed with "winning" that you lose sight of the people who helped you get there.

- **The Decision Filter:** "Does this increase my authority and impact, or is it a small-scale use of my energy?"

Heart's Desire 9: The Craving for Completion

Your soul is nourished by **Compassion and Universal Vision**. You are the humanitarian. You are driven by a need to help the collective and see the "big picture." You want your life to mean something for the entirety of humanity, not just yourself.

- **The Secret Hunger:** Total selflessness and the completion of cycles.

- **The Shadow:** Emotional burnout. You may take on the world's pain as your own, leading to a sense of profound sadness or resentment.

- **The Decision Filter:** "Does this serve the greater good, or is it purely for personal gain?"

V. The Master Soul Urges (11, 22, 33)

If your vowels sum to a Master Number, your internal hunger is "High Voltage." You are rarely satisfied with a mundane existence.

- **Soul Urge 11:** You crave **Illumination**. Your soul is hungry for spiritual or intuitive truth. You feel a constant, vibrating tension to be a "bridge" between the mundane and the extraordinary. You require a life of deep inspiration.

- **Soul Urge 22:** You crave **Large-Scale Construction**. You aren't satisfied with small projects. Your soul wants to build something that lasts for centuries. You require a life of immense, practical challenge.

- **Soul Urge 33:** You crave **Selfless Service**. This is the rarest urge. You are driven by a level of unconditional love that can be overwhelming. You require a life dedicated to healing and teaching others.

VI. The Conflict Analysis: When the Road Doesn't Match the Tank

The most significant impact of this chapter is identifying **Internal Friction**.

The Conflict: A Life Path 8 (working in high-finance) but with a Soul Urge 7 (craving quiet truth and solitude).

The Result: This person will be highly successful in the "8" world, but they will feel a persistent, gnawing sense of emptiness. They will reach the top of the mountain and wonder why they aren't happy.

The Solution: You must "feed" your Soul Urge separately from your Life Path. If you are an 8 Life Path with a 7 Soul Urge, you must schedule periods of absolute solitude and research to maintain your internal sanity, even as you pursue external power.

VII. Workbook: The Intrinsic Motivation Audit

Part 1: The Soul Calculation

Full Birth Name: ____

The Vowel Extraction:

1. **First Name Vowels:** _____ + _____ = Sum: _____ → Digit: _____
2. **Middle Name Vowels:** _____ + _____ = Sum: _____ → Digit: _____
3. **Last Name Vowels:** _____ + _____ = Sum: _____ → Digit: _____

Final Sum (1 + 2 + 3): _____ → **Your Heart's Desire Number:** _____

Part 2: The Procrastination Forensic

Think of a project you have been avoiding.

1. **The Project:** ____
2. **The Conflict:** How does this project violate your Heart's Desire? (e.g., "I'm avoiding this because my Soul Urge 5 hates the routine involved.")

   ____

   ____

   ____

3. **The Pivot:** How can you reframe this task to feed your Soul Urge? (e.g., "I will do the routine work in a new location to satisfy my 5's need for variety.")

   ____

   ____

   ____

Chapter 2: Determine Your Expression Number through Name Analysis

In the architecture of the self, if the **Life Path** is the road and the **Heart's Desire** is the fuel, then the **Expression Number** (often called the **Destiny Number**) is the **Vehicle**. It represents the sum total of your inherited capabilities, your physical and mental toolkits, and the natural talents you have at your disposal to navigate the journey. While your birth date was a cosmic "assignment," your name is your "equipment."

Calculating the Expression Number requires the integration of every letter in your full legal name at birth. This is because every sound—consonant and vowel alike—contributes to the structural integrity of your persona. In linguistics and physics, every letter vibrates at a specific frequency; when these frequencies are summed, they create the "Total Potential" of the individual. This chapter will guide you through the forensic calculation of your Expression and the psychological implications of your "Internal Equipment."

I. The Mechanics of Capacity: Vowels + Consonants

In Chapter 1, we isolated the vowels to find your internal "breath" or motivation. In this chapter, we add the consonants—the "bones" of your identity.

- **Vowels (Internal):** Your spiritual and emotional drives.
- **Consonants (External):** Your physical structure and social interface.
- **Total Expression (The Whole):** The functional reality of what you can achieve in the material world.

According to **Systems Theory**, the "whole is greater than the sum of its parts." Your Expression Number isn't just a list of traits; it is a **Functional Identity**. It dictates how you handle complexity, how you solve problems, and the "weight" you carry when you enter a room. If you have an Expression 8, you carry the "weight" of an executive or a builder, regardless of your current job title. If you have an Expression 3, you carry the "weight" of a communicator or an artist.

II. The Technical Calculation: The Pythagorean Matrix

To determine your Expression Number, we utilize the full **Pythagorean Alpha-Numeric Table**. Unlike the calculation for the Heart's Desire, we do not filter for specific letters; every character in your birth certificate name is converted into its numerical equivalent.

1. The Full Conversion Matrix

1	2	3	4	5	6	7	8	9
A	B	C	D	E	F	G	H	I
J	K	L	M	N	O	P	Q	R
S	T	U	V	W	X	Y	Z	

2. The Mathematical Reduction

We use the same reduction method established in Book 1, applying the Digital Root logic. Each name (First, Middle, Last) is summed and reduced individually before being combined into the final Expression.

The Formula:

$$E = \Sigma \,(\text{First}) + \Sigma \,(\text{Middle}) + \Sigma \,(\text{Last})$$

3. Step-by-Step Example: THOMAS ALVA EDISON

- **THOMAS:** T(2) + H(8) + O(6) + M(4) + A(1) + S(1) = 22 (Master Number, do not reduce yet).

- **ALVA:** A(1) + L(3) + V(4) + A(1) = 9

- **EDISON:** E(5) + D(4) + I(9) + S(1) + O(6) + N(5) = 30 → 3+0 = 3

- **Final Sum:** 22 + 9 + 3 = 34 → 3 + 4 = 7

- **Result:** Thomas Alva Edison has an **Expression 7**.

Note on Master Numbers: If an individual name sums to 11, 22, or 33, keep it as is until the final addition. This indicates that a specific part of your toolkit (like your surname/ancestry) carries "High-Voltage" potential.

III. The Expression Archetypes: Your Functional Toolkits

Your Expression Number defines the "Type" of vehicle you are driving. Understanding this allows you to stop forcing your vehicle to do things it wasn't designed for (e.g., trying to use a sports car to plow a field).

Expression 1: The Self-Propelled Leader

Your toolkit is designed for **pioneering**. You have the mental "hardware" to start new projects, work independently, and stand your ground.

- **Capabilities:** Decisiveness, original thinking, and high physical stamina.

- **The Vehicle:** A high-speed, single-seat interceptor. Built for speed and individual targets.

- **Psychological Edge:** You possess the "Conscientiousness" trait (from the Big Five) in the domain of self-directed goals.

Expression 2: The Adaptive Mediator

Your toolkit is designed for **cooperation**. You have a natural ability to see both sides of an issue and to function as the "glue" in a group.

- **Capabilities:** Diplomacy, attention to detail, and intuitive listening.

- **The Vehicle:** A high-tech satellite or communication hub. Built for reception and relaying information.

- **Psychological Edge:** High "Agreeableness" and "Empathy" that allows for seamless integration into social systems.

Expression 3: The Creative Catalyst

Your toolkit is designed for **expression**. You have a natural facility with words, art, or social engagement. You are designed to make things "move" through inspiration.

- **Capabilities:** Verbal dexterity, optimism, and social charisma.

- **The Vehicle:** A vibrant, open-top convertible. Built to be seen and to attract attention.

- **Psychological Edge:** High "Extraversion" and "Openness to Experience," facilitating rapid creative output.

Expression 4: The Master Architect

Your toolkit is designed for **foundation**. You possess the focus required to handle repetitive tasks, complex logistics, and long-term planning.

- **Capabilities:** Discipline, practical logic, and systemic organization.

- **The Vehicle:** A heavy-duty construction vehicle or tank. Built for durability and moving heavy loads over long distances.

- **Psychological Edge:** High "Conscientiousness" in the domain of order and reliability.

Expression 5: The Versatile Explorer

Your toolkit is designed for **adaptation**. You are the "Swiss Army Knife" of the numbers. You can learn almost anything quickly and pivot when circumstances change.

- **Capabilities:** Multitasking, public relations, and rapid learning.

- **The Vehicle:** An all-terrain vehicle (ATV). Built for changing landscapes and high-speed pivots.

- **Psychological Edge:** High "Openness" and "Neuroplasticity," allowing for quick recovery from environmental shifts.

Expression 6: The Harmonious Provider

Your toolkit is designed for **service**. You have a natural ability to manage people, foster a sense of "family," and improve the aesthetics of your environment.

- **Capabilities:** Counseling, management, and artistic balance.

- **The Vehicle:** A reliable, high-capacity SUV. Built for safety, comfort, and carrying others.

- **Psychological Edge:** High "Nurturing" instincts and a "System-Level" sense of responsibility.

Expression 7: The Analytical Specialist

Your toolkit is designed for **depth.** You possess a specialized mind capable of high-level abstract thought, technical research, or spiritual inquiry.

- **Capabilities:** Critical thinking, observation, and technical mastery.

- **The Vehicle:** A deep-sea submarine or laboratory. Built for isolation and exploring the "depths" where others cannot go.

- **Psychological Edge:** High "Introspective Capacity" and a natural filter for superficial data.

Expression 8: The Executive Powerhouse

Your toolkit is designed for **manifestation.** You have the capacity to handle large amounts of money, people, and responsibility simultaneously.

- **Capabilities:** Financial acumen, leadership, and efficient resource management.

- **The Vehicle:** A massive freight train or a corporate jet. Built for massive momentum and global impact.

- **Psychological Edge:** High "Self-Efficacy" and the ability to view emotions as data points in a larger strategy.

Expression 9: The Universal Humanitarian

Your toolkit is designed for **breadth.** You have the ability to understand complex human systems and to finish what others have started.

- **Capabilities:** Global vision, teaching, and ending outdated cycles.

- **The Vehicle:** A global broadcasting station or an ocean liner. Built for wide-reaching impact and "ending" journeys.

- **Psychological Edge:** High "Compassion" and the ability to process "Collective Loss" or transition.

IV. Master Number Toolkits: 11, 22, 33

If your full name reduces to 11, 22, or 33, your "Vehicle" is a specialized, high-performance machine that requires more maintenance than the average.

- **Expression 11 (The Intuitive Transmitter):** You have a toolkit designed for high-level "downloads." You are a "lightning rod" for ideas. *Challenge:* Sensory overload and nervous tension.

- **Expression 22 (The Master Builder):** You have a toolkit designed for turning "Impossible Dreams" into concrete systems. You can manage vast complexities. *Challenge:* Overwhelming pressure and the fear of failure on a grand scale.

- **Expression 33 (The Master Teacher):** You have a toolkit designed for the complete emotional and spiritual elevation of others. *Challenge:* Self-sacrifice to the point of personal erosion.

V. Integration: The Road vs. The Vehicle

The most vital insight of this chapter is the **Expression-Path Interaction**.

- **The Life Path (Birth Date):** Where you are going (The Destination).

- **The Expression (Name):** What you are driving (The Vehicle).

Scenario A: The Harmonic Match

- *Life Path 8 (Success) + Expression 8 (Executive Capacity):* You are a freight train traveling on a heavy-duty track. You will achieve results with relative ease.

Scenario B: The Dissonant Match

- *Life Path 5 (Travel/Change) + Expression 4 (The Builder/Rigid):* You are a heavy-duty construction tank trying to race on a Formula 1 track. You will find the "constant change" of the 5 path exhausting because your "4 vehicle" is built for slow, methodical stability.

Understanding this mismatch allows you to perform a **"Psychological Retrofit."** If you are a 4 Vehicle on a 5 Road, you must build "Mobile Structures"—systems that allow you to maintain your need for order while moving at high speed.

Workbook: The Expression Audit

Part 1: Calculation

Full Birth Name: ____

The Summation:

1. First Name Total: __________ → Reduced: ________________

2. Middle Name Total: _______ → Reduced: ________________

3. Last Name Total: __________ → Reduced: ________________

Final Expression Number: _____

Part 2: Capability Audit

List 3 skills that come to you so easily you often forget they are talents.

    1. ____

    2. ____

    3. ____

How do these skills align with your Expression Archetype (e.g., The Architect, The Explorer, The Mediator)?

Part 3: The "Road vs. Vehicle" Check

Write down your Life Path Number (Book 1) and your Expression Number (Book 2).

- **Life Path:** ____

- **Expression:** ____

- **The Analysis:** On a scale of 1-10, how well does your "Vehicle" fit your "Road"? If the score is low, what is one "Modification" you can make to your toolkit to handle the terrain better?

    ____

    ____

    ____

Chapter 3: Project Your Personality Number to Shape Your Public Image

If the Heart's Desire is your engine's fuel and the Expression is your vehicle's chassis, the Personality Number is the paint job, the bodywork, and the User Interface (UI). It is the most "external" of your core numbers. While it may seem superficial compared to the deep cravings of the soul, the Personality Number is functionally vital: it is the "Social Mask" that filters your interactions with the world.

In the Pythagorean system, the Personality Number is calculated using only the **consonants** of your full legal name at birth. In linguistic terms, consonants provide the structure, the hard edges, and the "container" for the breath of the vowels. Metaphysically, they represent the physical shell you inhabit and the first impression you project onto others. This chapter will analyze how to calibrate this mask to ensure your public image is an asset that accurately represents—rather than obscures—your internal truth.

I. The Social Mask: Necessity vs. Inauthenticity

There is a common misconception that having a "mask" is a form of deception. In social psychology, specifically the work of **Erving Goffman**, this is referred to as "Impression Management." Goffman argued that social life is a theatrical performance, and to function effectively, we must adopt a "front-stage" persona.

Your Personality Number is your natural "front-stage" script. It dictates:

1. **The First Impression:** What people assume about you before you speak.

2. **The Protective Filter:** How much of your "Internal Self" you allow strangers to see.

3. **Social Expectations:** The role society instinctively asks you to play (e.g., the Leader, the Comforter, the Expert).

When your Personality Number is in alignment with your Life Path and Soul Urge, you experience **Social Fluidity**. People "get" you quickly. When there is a mismatch—for example, a Soul Urge 8 (Powerful) with a Personality 2 (Gentle)—you may feel constantly underestimated or misunderstood, leading to "System Exhaustion" as you repeatedly have to correct people's perceptions of you.

II. The Technical Calculation: The Structural Shell

To find your Personality Number, we return to the Pythagorean matrix, but we strip away the vowels (A, E, I, O, U) and the "vocalic Y." We are left with the "Bones" of the name.

1. The Consonant Conversion Table

1	2	3	4	5	6	7	8	9
	B	C	D		F	G	H	
J	K	L	M	N		P	Q	R
S	T		V	W	X		Z	

2. The Methodology

Write your full legal name. Cross out the vowels. Assign the numerical values to the remaining consonants. Sum and reduce each name (First, Middle, Last) individually before finding the final total.

The Digital Root Formula for Consonants (C):

$$P = \sum C_{first} + \sum C_{middle} + \sum C_{last} \quad (\mathrm{mod}\ 9)$$

(Remember: Master Numbers 11 and 22 are not reduced in the sub-totals).

Example: SAMUEL MARK TWAIN

- **SAMUEL (S, M, L):** $1 + 4 + 3 = 8$
- **MARK (M, R, K):** $4 + 9 + 2 = 15 \rightarrow 1 + 5 = 6$
- **TWAIN (T, W, N):** $2 + 5 + 5 = 12 \rightarrow 1 + 2 = 3$
- **Final Sum:** $8 + 6 + 3 = 17 \rightarrow 1 + 7 = 8$
- *Result: The Personality Number is 8 (The Executive/Professional Mask).*

III. The Personality Archetypes: Your Social UI

Personality 1: The Commanding Professional

You project an aura of independence, confidence, and self-reliance. Even if you are feeling nervous internally, the world sees a person who is in control.

- **The Appearance:** Sharp, clean-cut, or distinct. You often look like you are "on a mission."
- **The Social Perception:** People see you as a leader or a "loner" who doesn't need help.
- **The Risk:** You can appear unapproachable or "too busy" for others, discouraging collaboration.

Personality 2: The Gentle Diplomat

You project an aura of warmth, approachability, and peace. People naturally feel safe sharing their secrets with you within minutes of meeting.

- **The Appearance:** Soft colors, comfortable but neat attire. You look "easy on the eyes."

- **The Social Perception:** People see you as a listener, a mediator, or a supportive partner.
- **The Risk:** People may perceive your kindness as weakness, attempting to overstep your boundaries.

Personality 3: The Radiant Socialite

You project an aura of joy, creativity, and charisma. You are the "spark" in the room. People expect you to entertain or lighten the mood.

- **The Appearance:** Stylish, colorful, or artistic. You likely have a memorable smile or expressive eyes.
- **The Social Perception:** People see you as fun, witty, and optimistic.
- **The Risk:** People may not take you seriously in professional settings, assuming you lack "depth" because you are so expressive.

Personality 4: The Reliable Pillar

You project an aura of stability, honesty, and common sense. You look like the person who knows where the emergency exits are.

- **The Appearance:** Practical, traditional, and high-quality. You prefer "classic" over "trendy."
- **The Social Perception:** People see you as the "Adult in the Room." They trust you with their keys and their money.
- **The Risk:** You can appear rigid, boring, or overly cautious to more "High-Voltage" numbers.

Personality 5: The Magnetic Adventurer

You project an aura of excitement, sensuality, and wit. You look like you just got back from a trip or are about to leave for one.

- **The Appearance:** Trendy, eclectic, and designed for movement. You likely have a "restless" energy.
- **The Social Perception:** People see you as clever, adaptable, and "cool."
- **The Risk:** You can appear unreliable or "flaky" to those who value long-term stability.

Personality 6: The Gracious Caretaker

You project an aura of motherly/fatherly warmth, responsibility, and comfort. You look like "Home."

- **The Appearance:** Groomed, welcoming, and harmonious. You often carry an air of "Old World" manners.

- **The Social Perception:** People instinctively come to you for advice or nurturing.

- **The Risk:** You can appear "smothering" or overly judgmental if others don't meet your standards of harmony.

Personality 7: The Mysterious Sage

You project an aura of intellect, observation, and reserve. You look like you are "watching the watchers."

- **The Appearance:** Dignified, often understated or "intellectual" (glasses, dark colors). You have a "poker face."

- **The Social Perception:** People see you as wise, mysterious, or perhaps "odd." They are often a bit intimidated by your silence.

- **The Risk:** You can appear arrogant or cold, even when you are simply lost in thought.

Personality 8: The Power Player

You project an aura of success, authority, and material competence. You look like you own the building (or should).

- **The Appearance:** "Power dressing." You wear clothes that signal status and quality.

- **The Social Perception:** People see you as a boss or an authority figure. They expect you to pay the check and make the decisions.

- **The Risk:** You can appear domineering or obsessed with status, making it hard for people to connect with you emotionally.

Personality 9: The Wise Humanitarian

You project an aura of global wisdom, tolerance, and "agelessness." You often look older when young and younger when old.

- **The Appearance:** Sophisticated, perhaps "bohemian" or world-traveler style.

- **The Social Perception:** People see you as someone who has "seen it all." They look to you for the big-picture perspective.

- **The Risk:** You can appear detached or "too holy" for the mundane details of daily life.

IV. Calibration: Solving the Personality-Soul Gap

The greatest source of social friction occurs when your **Personality (The Mask)** and your **Heart's Desire (The Soul)** are in a "dissonant" relationship.

The Underestimation Trap:

- *Soul Urge 8 (Power) + Personality 2 (Gentle).*

- **The Result:** You crave authority and mastery, but the world sees a "helper." You find yourself constantly having to assert your power because people don't expect it from your "UI."

The Overestimation Trap:

- *Soul Urge 2 (Peace) + Personality 8 (Power).*

- **The Result:** You crave quiet partnership and harmony, but the world treats you like a CEO. You are constantly handed responsibilities you don't actually want because you "look" like you can handle them.

Strategic Calibration:

To minimize "System Leakage," you must use your Personality Number as a **Tool.** If you have a Personality 7 (Reserved) but a Life Path 3 (Communicator), you must consciously use your "Mystery" to create "Curation." Don't fight the mask; use the mask to protect the internal frequency.

V. The Shadow of the Mask

Every Personality Number has a "Shadow" state—usually triggered by stress or the fear of social rejection.

- **The 1 Shadow:** Aggression and bullying.

- **The 4 Shadow:** Stubbornness and "Wall-building."

- **The 7 Shadow:** Complete social withdrawal and paranoia.

When you are in your Shadow Personality, your "UI" becomes "Glitchy." People stop trusting your presentation because the "mask" is no longer a bridge; it has become a "barrier."

VI. Workbook: The Personality Audit

Part 1: Calculation

Full Birth Name: ____________________________________

Consonants Only:

1. First Name Consonants → Sum: ____ →Reduced: ________
2. Middle Name Consonants→ Sum: →Reduced: __________
3. Last Name Consonants → Sum: ____ →Reduced: ________

Final Personality Number: _____________________________

Part 2: The Social Reflection

Ask three people who don't know you intimately to describe you in three words.

- **Person 1:** ____________, ____________, ___________
- **Person 2:** ____________, ____________, ___________
- **Person 3:** ____________, ____________, ___________

The Comparison: How do these descriptions align with your Personality Number archetype? Are they describing your "Mask" or your "Soul"?

Part 3: The UI Refinement

If your Personality Number and Soul Urge are in conflict (e.g., 8 vs. 2), what is one physical change (style, posture, communication speed) you can make to "Bridge" the gap?

____

____

____

Chapter 4: Balance Conflicting Numbers within Your Personal Profile

In the preceding chapters, we dissected the individual components of your numerical anatomy: your internal cravings (**Heart's Desire**), your natural capabilities (**Expression**), and your social interface (**Personality**). In Book 1, we established your primary trajectory (**Life Path**). If you were a simple machine, these numbers would all hum at the same frequency. However, human beings are complex, multi-layered systems—often described by psychologists as "walking contradictions."

Chapter 4 is the most critical stage of your self-audit. This is where we move from data collection to **Systems Integration**. We will analyze **Numerical Friction**—the internal tension that arises when your core numbers are out of "Phase." This dissonance is not a defect; it is the source of your greatest psychological complexity and, if managed through the "Internal Peace Treaty" protocol, it becomes the catalyst for your greatest evolution.

I. The Physics of Personal Dissonance: Wave Interference

In the physical world, every sound and light wave operates on a frequency. When two waves meet, they interact through a process called **Interference**.

1. **Constructive Interference:** When the peaks of two waves align (F1 + F2), the amplitude increases. In your profile, this feels like "Flow." You want to lead (1), and you have the tools to lead (1).

2. **Destructive Interference:** When the peak of one wave meets the trough of another, they cancel each other out. This is where your numbers "clash." You want freedom (5), but you feel a heavy responsibility to stay put (4 or 6).

Mathematically, we can view your total identity as a composite wave function:

$$\psi \text{ Total} = \psi \text{ LifePath} + \psi \text{ SoulUrge} + \psi \text{ Expression}$$

If the phase shift Φ between these variables is too great, the resulting identity ψ becomes unstable, leading to what psychologists call **Cognitive Dissonance**. This is the mental discomfort experienced by a person who holds two or more contradictory beliefs or values at the same time. In your blueprint, this isn't just a belief; it is a structural misalignment of your "User Interface" and your "Core Engine."

II. Mapping the "Core Four" Interaction Matrix

To resolve conflict, we must first perform a forensic mapping of where the friction is occurring. Use the following table to identify the "Pressure Points" in your current life stage.

Interaction Pairing	The Psychological Domain	Symptom of Dissonance
Life Path (LP) vs. Heart's Desire (HD)	Action vs. Motivation	You are "successful" by world standards but feel a deep, gnawing emptiness or boredom.
Heart's Desire (HD) vs. Personality (P)	Soul vs. Mask	You feel like a "fraud." People love a version of you that doesn't actually exist.

Interaction Pairing	The Psychological Domain	Symptom of Dissonance
Expression (E) vs. Life Path (LP)	Tools vs. Direction	You have the right goal, but every task feels like "pushing a boulder uphill" because it's not your natural talent.
Expression (E) vs. Personality (P)	Capacity vs. Projection	People either underestimate your intelligence or overestimate your confidence based on how you "look."

III. Advanced Archetypes of Internal Conflict

Most human suffering is not caused by external events, but by the internal "civil war" between these numbers. Below are the most frequent high-friction archetypes discovered in clinical behavioral analysis.

1. The Reluctant Executive (8 LP vs. 2/9 HD)

- o **The Blueprint:** You are on a path of material power and management (8), but your soul craves intimacy (2) or universal compassion (9).
- o **The Conflict:** You are excellent at making money or running a team, but you feel "guilty" about your success. You may sabotage your own authority to remain "likable."
- o **The Integration:** You must adopt the **"conscious capitalist"** model. Use the 8's power as a vehicle to deliver the 9's compassion. Your "Why" (9) justifies the "How" (8).

2. The Anchor and the Sail (4 LP vs. 5 HD)

- o **The Blueprint:** You are built for stability and process (4), but you hunger for total freedom and variety (5).
- o **The Conflict:** This is the most common cause of "Mid-Life Crisis." You build a perfect, stable life (4) only to feel like a prisoner in it.
- o **The Integration:** You require **"Mobile Stability."** You must build structures (4) that are specifically designed to be portable or that fund "scheduled chaos" (5).

3. The Invisible Visionary (11 LP vs. 4/7 P)

- o **The Blueprint:** You have a high-voltage, intuitive Life Path (11), but your social mask is logical, reserved, or pragmatic (4 or 7).
- o **The Conflict:** You have world-changing ideas, but you look so "normal" or "stoic" that no one ever asks for your opinion. You feel "stuck" in a mundane mask while your soul is on fire.
- o **The Integration:** Use the **Socratic Bridge**. Use your 4/7 logic to provide evidence and structure for your 11 visions. This makes your "weird" ideas palatable to a logical world.

4. The Tortured Humanitarian (9 LP vs. 1/8 HD)

- o **The Blueprint:** Your path is to serve the collective (9), but your internal drive is for personal achievement and recognition (1 or 8).
- o **The Conflict:** You feel like a "hypocrite" because you want to help people, but you also want to be the one in charge and get all the credit.
- o **The Integration:** Accept that **effective altruism requires leadership.** Your need for personal mastery (1/8) is the very tool that makes your humanitarian work (9) scalable.

IV. The Biological Impact:
Polyvagal Theory & Numerical Stress

When your numbers are in conflict, your body stays in a state of "High Alert." According to **Dr. Stephen Porges' Polyvagal Theory**, our nervous system is constantly scanning for "neuroception" of safety or threat.

- o **Resonance (Alignment):** Your body stays in the **Ventral Vagal** state—social engagement, creativity, and digestion.
- o **Dissonance (Conflict):** Your body shifts into **Sympathetic Activation** (Anxiety/Fight/Flight) or **Dorsal Vagal** (Shutdown/Depression).

If you have a Personality 3 (Social/Expressive) but a Soul Urge 7 (Solitary/Reserved), forcing yourself to attend a networking event is literally interpreted by your nervous system as a threat. You aren't "socially anxious"; you are experiencing **Numerical Dissonance**. Understanding this allows you to stop shaming yourself for your physiological reactions and start managing your "System Load."

V. The "Internal Peace Treaty" Protocol

To move from friction to flow, you must facilitate a negotiation between your numbers. We use a four-step synthesis protocol based on **Systems Thinking**.

Step 1: The Sovereignty Audit

Acknowledge that no number is "wrong." In **Bloom's Taxonomy**, the highest level of learning is "Evaluation." You must evaluate each number for its specific utility.

- *Task:* List each of your numbers and write one thing you are "grateful" for regarding that frequency. (e.g., "I am grateful for my 4 because it keeps my taxes paid, even though my 5 hates the paperwork.")

Step 2: The "Zoning" Method

If two numbers are in high conflict, don't try to merge them; **zone** them by time and space.

- *The Protocol:* Assign specific domains of your life to specific numbers. Your "7" gets the hours between 9 PM and 7 AM (Silence/Study). Your "3" gets the social hours. Your "8" handles the bank account. Do not let the "3" make financial decisions, and do not let the "8" handle your spiritual retreats.

Step 3: Somatic Verification

When faced with a choice, "Ask the Body." Resonance feels like an expansion in the chest. Dissonance feels like a contraction in the solar plexus. If you feel a contraction, ask: "Which part of my blueprint am I betraying right now?"

Step 4: The Resource Exchange

Ask: "What does Number A need from Number B to feel safe?"

> **Example:** If your 5 (Freedom) wants to quit your job, your 4 (Security) will panic. The "Peace Treaty" is: The 5 can quit *once* the 4 has seen a bank statement with six months of runway. Once the 4 is safe, the 5 is truly free to fly without the "biological brakes" of anxiety.

VI. Workbook: The Socratic Synthesis Audit

Complete these exercises to finalize your Internal Peace Treaty.

Exercise 1: The Civil War Map

Which two numbers in your profile feel like they are currently "sabotaging" each other?

1. ______________________________ (Number A)
2. ______________________________ (Number B)

> *How does the sabotage manifest? (e.g., "I work hard all day (4) but then spend all my money on travel (5) and feel guilty.")*

Exercise 2: The Socratic "Bridge" Question

Using the work of **Paul & Elder**, ask a deep question to bridge the gap: "How can my [Number A] provide the necessary resources for my [Number B] to flourish without fear?"

____

____

____

Exercise 3: The Boundary Commitment

What is one "Zone" you will establish this week to protect a suppressed number? (e.g., "I will spend Tuesday nights alone to feed my 7, no matter how much my 3 wants to go out.")

____

____

____

Chapter 5: Strengthen Your Emotional Intelligence Using Personal Blueprints

Emotional Intelligence (EI) is frequently cited as the single most important predictor of success in the 21st century. While traditional IQ measures your cognitive processing speed—the raw power of your "CPU"—EI measures your ability to perceive, control, and evaluate emotions. However, most EI training is fundamentally flawed because it is "one-size-fits-all." It suggests that everyone should manage anger or seek motivation through the same generic affirmations.

In this chapter, we pivot from generic psychological advice to **Personalized Emotional Intelligence**. We use your numerical blueprint to identify your specific emotional "Triggers" and "Resolutions." We define EI through a specialized numerical lens:

$$EI = \left(\frac{\text{Self-Awareness}}{\text{Self-Regulation}} \right) \times \text{Alignment}$$

By the end of this chapter, you will no longer view your emotions as random biological storms. Instead, you will see them as **Somatic Notifications** sent from your blueprint to alert you of an alignment—or a misalignment—with your core frequency.

I. The Anatomy of Emotional Intelligence: A Pythagorean Framework

Using the framework established by **Daniel Goleman**, we can map the core pillars of Emotional Intelligence directly onto your Pythagorean profile. This isn't just about "being nice"; it's about the efficient management of your internal energy.

1. Self-Awareness: The Internal Dashboard

Self-awareness is the ability to recognize a feeling as it happens. Through the lens of Book 2, this means recognizing which part of your profile is currently "speaking." When you feel a surge of frustration, is it your **Life Path** (The Road) hitting a roadblock, or is it your **Soul Urge** (The Fuel) being contaminated by external expectations? High-EI individuals use their numbers as a diagnostic tool.

2. Self-Regulation: Managing the "High-Voltage"

Self-regulation is the "Circuit Breaker" of the human psyche. Certain numbers carry more "Voltage" than others—specifically Master Numbers 11, 22, and 33. If you do not understand the structural reality of your blueprint, you might misdiagnose structural "tension" as clinical anxiety. Self-regulation in numerology is the act of consciously "Stepping Down" the voltage so it doesn't fry your social or physical systems.

3. Motivation: Feeding the Intrinsic Engine

As established in Chapter 1, motivation is the domain of the Soul Urge. High-EI individuals do not "wait" to be inspired; they consciously "feed" their Soul Urge to generate intrinsic drive. If you are a Soul Urge 5, you find motivation through variety and sensory input; if you are a Soul Urge 4, you find it through progress tracking and the slow build.

4. Empathy: The Numerical Social X-Ray

Empathy is the ability to recognize emotions in others. Once you understand your own blueprint, you begin to see the "Numerical Archetypes" in the people around you. You stop taking people's behavior personally. You realize that your partner isn't "lazy"—they may be a Life Path 7 who requires a different kind of mental processing time than you do as a Life Path 1.

5. Social Skills: UI Calibration

Social skills are the strategic application of your **Personality Number.** This is the ability to use your "Social Mask" to achieve a desired outcome without betraying your core authenticity. It is the bridge between your internal truth and external harmony.

II. The Somatic Connection: Polyvagal Theory in Practice

To truly master EI, we must look at the body. According to **Dr. Stephen Porges' Polyvagal Theory,** our nervous system is constantly scanning the environment for safety. Your numerical blueprint dictates what your body considers "Safe" versus "Threatening."

- **The Ventral Vagal State (The Green Zone):** This is where your numbers are "In Phase." You feel social, curious, and creative. If you are a 3 Expression, you are talking and creating. If you are a 4, your desk is organized.

- **The Sympathetic State (The Red Zone):** This is the "Fight or Flight" response. It occurs when a core number is blocked. For a 1, this is triggered by a loss of autonomy. For a 6, it's triggered by discord in the home.

- **The Dorsal Vagal State (The Blue Zone):** This is "Shutdown." This happens when you have suppressed your core numbers for too long to satisfy your "Mask" (Personality). You feel numb, depressed, or unmotivated.

The EI Protocol: When you feel a physical sensation—tightness in the chest, a knot in the stomach—ask: *"Which number in my blueprint is being silenced?"*

III. The Shadow and the Light: A Regulatory Guide

Every number in your profile has a "Light" (High-EI/Aligned) state and a "Shadow" (Low-EI/Reactive) state. Use the following table to calibrate your emotional responses.

Number	The Emotional Trigger	The Shadow Reaction	The High-EI Resolution
1	Micromanagement	Aggression / Bullying	Initiate a solo project
2	Criticism / Discord	Passive-aggression	State needs clearly and set a boundary
3	Being ignored / Boredom	Gossiping / Over-sharing	Channel energy into a creative outlet
4	Chaos / Unreliability	Rigidity / Judgment	Create a micro-system for the chaos
5	Restrictions / Routine	Recklessness / Escapism	Schedule "Planned Chaos" or travel
6	Ingratitude	Martyrdom / Interference	Practice self-care and release the "fix"
7	Superficiality / Noise	Coldness / Withdrawal	Retreat into silence for deep study
8	Lack of progress	Ruthlessness / Greed	Re-evaluate the system, not the person
9	Injustice / Small-mindedness	Preachiness / Burnout	Focus on one tangible act of service

IV. Master Number Emotional Management: High-Voltage Regulation

If your blueprint contains **11, 22, or 33**, you are dealing with "High-Voltage" emotional equipment. These numbers act as massive transformers; they receive more "input" than mundane numbers and, therefore, require a specialized "cooling system."

- **The 11 (The Intuitive):** Your EI challenge is **Sensory Overload**. You feel everything. High EI for an 11 is learning to distinguish between your emotions and the "static" of the room.

- **The 22 (The Architect):** Your EI challenge is **Overwhelming Pressure**. You feel the weight of building the future. High EI for a 22 is learning that "Rome wasn't built in a day" and managing the somatic stress of massive projects.

- **The 33 (The Teacher):** Your EI challenge is **Emotional Martyrdom**. You feel responsible for everyone's healing. High EI for a 33 is knowing when to close the "Emotional Clinic" and nurture yourself.

V. Decoding Others: The Empathy X-Ray

The final stage of Emotional Intelligence is the ability to de-escalate others. You can use your knowledge of archetypes to "decode" the difficult people in your life.

1. **The "Angry" Boss (Likely 1 or 8):** They aren't trying to be mean; they are frustrated by a lack of progress or autonomy. **EI Response:** Provide a status update and show competence.

2. **The "Sensitive" Partner (Likely 2 or 6):** They aren't trying to be needy; they are scanning for harmony. **EI Response:** Offer verbal appreciation and a calm environment.

3. **The "Detached" Colleague (Likely 7):** They aren't being arrogant; they are processing data. **EI Response:** Give them space and ask for their "analysis" later.

By moving from **Judgment** ("They are annoying") to **Forensic Observation** ("They are vibrating at a 7 frequency"), you remove the emotional charge from the interaction. You are no longer fighting people; you are interacting with frequencies.

VI. Workbook: The Emotional Intelligence Audit

Part 1: The Trigger Map

Identify a recurring negative emotion you felt this week.

- **The Emotion:** ____

- **The Trigger:** What happened immediately before? _________

- **The Blueprint Link:** Which of your numbers was "Blocked" or "Offended"? ____

Part 2: The Regulatory Pivot

Using the table in Section III, what is the "High-EI Resolution" for that specific number?

- The Action: ____

Part 3: The Somatic Check-In

Sit in silence for 2 minutes. Where do you feel tension in your body?

- **The Location:** ____

- **The Translation:** If that body part could speak for one of your numbers, what would it say? (e.g., "My throat is tight because my 3 wants to speak up.")

____

____

____

Conclusion: Synthesize the Core Elements of Your Internal Identity

We have reached the terminal point of **Book 2: The Internal Audit.**

If Book 1 was a study of the "Where"—your Life Path, your trajectory, and the terrain you are destined to cross—Book 2 has been a relentless deep dive into the "Who." We have acted as forensic accountants of the soul, stripping away the layers of social conditioning to reveal the mechanical truth of your internal architecture. We have examined the **Heart's Desire** (your fuel), analyzed the **Expression Number** (your vehicle), and audited the **Personality Number** (your interface). We have looked at where these numbers conflict, where they harmonize, and how they trigger your emotional nervous system.

But analysis without synthesis is merely deconstruction. You can take a watch apart and name every gear and spring, but until you put it back together in perfect alignment, it cannot tell time. To conclude this journey, we must now move from the "Audit" phase to the **"Synthesis"** phase.

In the world of systems engineering, synthesis is the process of combining diverse elements into a unified whole that functions more effectively than its individual parts. In the context of your Pythagorean blueprint, synthesis means no longer looking at your numbers as a list of separate, competing ingredients, but as a single, coherent **Internal Identity**.

This conclusion is not just a summary; it is an integration manual. It is designed to help you merge the contradictory aspects of your nature into a "Unified Field" of self, allowing you to move into Book 3 (The External World) as a whole person rather than a fragmented one.

I. The Theory of the Unified Self: Moving Beyond Fragmentation

In theoretical physics, scientists have spent decades searching for a "Unified Field Theory"—a single mathematical framework that can explain gravity, electromagnetism, and nuclear forces simultaneously. In psychology, specifically in the work of **Carl Jung**, the equivalent goal is **Individuation.**

Individuation is the process of becoming who you were inherently designed to be. It is the act of gathering the fragmented pieces of the psyche—the persona, the shadow, the ego, and the self—and forging them into an unbreakable whole.

For most of your life, you have likely operated in a state of **Structural Fragmentation**.

- **At work**, you might be operating strictly from your **Expression Number** (using your talents to earn a paycheck) while starving your Heart's Desire.

- **In relationships**, you might be operating strictly from your **Personality Number** (acting the way you think a "good partner" acts) while suppressing your true needs.

- **In solitude**, you might finally feel your **Heart's Desire**, but feel powerless to enact it because you haven't integrated your Life Path's trajectory.

This fragmentation is the root cause of what we call "existential exhaustion." It takes an immense amount of caloric and psychic energy to keep these different versions of yourself separate. Synthesis is the act of collapsing these walls. When you are synthesized, you are the same person in the boardroom as you are in the bedroom. Your "Fuel" (Heart's Desire) powers your "Vehicle" (Expression), which is protected by your "Paint Job" (Personality), all driving down the "Road" (Life Path).

II. The Forensic Review:
The Three Pillars of Your Identity

Before we lock the pieces together, let us perform one final, high-definition review of the components we are synthesizing. We must view them now not as static numbers, but as **Dynamic Forces.**

1. The Heart's Desire: The Force of Volition

Your Heart's Desire (calculated from the vowels) is your **Force of Volition.** It is the only part of you that is truly "Autotelic"—meaning it possesses its own purpose within itself.

- **The Synthesis Function:** In the unified self, the Heart's Desire acts as the **Thermostat.** It dictates the temperature of your life. If the Heart's Desire is cold, no amount of external success (Life Path achievement) will make the life feel warm.

- **The Warning:** If you synthesize your life around your wallet instead of your vowels, the system will eventually crash via "Mid-Life Crisis."

2. The Expression: The Force of Capability

Your Expression Number (calculated from the full name) is your **Force of Capability.** It is the sum total of your biological and intellectual inheritance.

- **The Synthesis Function:** In the unified self, the Expression acts as the **Transmission.** It translates the raw energy of the soul (Heart's Desire) into torque that moves you forward in the physical world.

- **The Warning:** If you try to drive a vehicle that doesn't match your transmission (e.g., trying to be a detailed accountant with a creative Expression 3), you will strip the gears. Synthesis requires accepting your limitations as much as your talents.

3. The Personality: The Force of Protection

Your Personality Number (calculated from the consonants) is your **Force of Protection.** It is the selective membrane that decides what gets in and what gets out.

- **The Synthesis Function:** In the unified self, the Personality acts as the **User Interface (UI).** It is designed to lower friction in social interactions so that your deeper numbers can do their work without interference.

- **The Warning:** In a fragmented self, the Personality becomes a prison wall. In a synthesized self, it is a gate. You hold the key, and you decide when to open it.

III. The Architecture of Alignment: Three Critical Integrations

How do we actually perform the welding? We must look at the three critical "joints" where these numbers meet. If there is weakness in the system, it will always be found at these intersections.

Joint 1: The Soul-to-Tool Alignment (Heart's Desire + Expression)

The Question: *"Do I have the tools to give my soul what it wants?"*

This is the most common source of professional frustration. You know *what* you want (Soul), but you feel you lack the *talent* to get it (Expression).

- **The Scenario:** Consider a subject with a **Heart's Desire 1** (Craving Leadership/Innovation) but an **Expression 2** (Designed for Diplomacy/Support).

- **The Friction:** The soul screams "Lead! Go alone!" but the toolkit says "Wait, let's ask for permission. Let's work together." This person feels like a lion trapped in the body of a lamb.

- **The Synthesis:** The synthesis here is **"The Diplomatic Leader."** This person must stop trying to lead like an 8 (bulldozer) or a 1 (warrior). They must realize that their *method* of leadership is consensus-building. They satisfy the Soul's need for autonomy by creating their own team, but they use the Expression's talent for harmony to run that team.

- **The Protocol:** You must rewrite your job description. Does your daily activity utilize your Expression number? If yes, does the *outcome* of that activity feed your Heart's Desire? If the answer to either is "No," the system is out of alignment.

Joint 2: The Soul-to-Social Alignment (Heart's Desire + Personality)

The Question: *"Does the world see who I actually am?"*

This is the most common source of social isolation. You feel misunderstood because your "advertisement" (Personality) doesn't match the "product" (Soul).

- **The Scenario:** Consider a subject with a **Heart's Desire 7** (Craving Silence/Wisdom) but a **Personality 3** (The Life of the Party).

- **The Friction:** Because they look like a 3, people constantly invite them to parties, expect them to be funny, and interrupt them. The 7 Soul is exhausted and feels invaded. The person feels "fake" because they perform joy while feeling drained.

- **The Synthesis:** The synthesis here is **"The Curated Socialite."** This person must use the 3 Personality as a *tool*, not a default setting. They turn on the charm for 2 hours to network, and then they use that same charm to gracefully exit: "I have loved seeing you, and now I must vanish to recharge." They use the social skill to protect the solitude, rather than letting the social skill destroy the solitude.

Joint 3: The Tool-to-Road Alignment (Expression + Life Path)

The Question: *"Is my vehicle built for this terrain?"*

This is the most common source of burnout. You are driving a Ferrari on a dirt road, or a tank on a racetrack.

- **The Scenario:** A **Life Path 5** (The Road of Freedom and Chaos) with an **Expression 4** (The Toolkit of Structure and Routine).

- **The Friction:** The Life Path keeps throwing unexpected changes, travel, and instability at the person. The Expression 4 panics because it wants to build a spreadsheet and stay home. The person feels constant anxiety.

- **The Synthesis:** The synthesis is **"The Mobile Fortress."** The person must use their 4 skills to build systems that *allow* for the 5's movement. They create a rigid routine *for* travel. They have a strict financial plan that *funds* the chaos. They don't stop the movement (Life Path), but they build a roll-cage (Expression) to survive it.

IV. The "Internal Peace Treaty" as an Operating System

In Chapter 4, we drafted an "Internal Peace Treaty" to resolve specific conflicts. As we conclude Book 2, this treaty must graduate from a temporary fix to a permanent **Operating System (OS)**.

Synthesis requires a shift in cognitive framework from **Binary Thinking** to **Quantum Thinking.**

- **Binary Thinking (Fragmented):** "I am either a spiritual person (7) OR a wealthy person (8). I cannot be both."
- **Quantum Thinking (Synthesized):** "I am a system that requires material resources (8) to fund spiritual research (7)."

To maintain this synthesis, you must adopt the role of the **CEO of Self.** In a corporation, the CFO (Chief Financial Officer) often disagrees with the Creative Director. The CFO wants to save money; the Creative Director wants to spend it. The CEO does not fire either of them. The CEO integrates their needs: "We will spend the money (Creative) on the projects with the highest ROI (Financial)."

You are the CEO.

- Your **Heart's Desire** is your Creative Director (Vision).
- Your **Expression** is your COO (Operations).
- Your **Personality** is your PR Director (Public Image).
- Your **Life Path** is the Board of Directors (The mandate you must fulfill).

When you feel internal conflict, do not ask "What is wrong with me?" Ask: *"Which department is unhappy, and what resources do they need?"*

V. The Somatic Signature of Synthesis: Polyvagal Confirmation

How do you know, empirically, that you have achieved synthesis? You cannot measure it with a ruler, but you can measure it with your nervous system.

Throughout this book, we have referenced the **Polyvagal Theory.** We end with it because the body is the ultimate truth-teller. A fragmented identity lives in a state of chronic **Sympathetic Activation** (low-grade anxiety) or **Dorsal Shutdown** (low-grade depression). It takes enormous biological effort to pretend to be someone you are not.

The Somatic Signature of Synthesis is "Flow." In psychology, Flow (defined by Mihaly Csikszentmihalyi) is a state where action and awareness merge. When your numbers are synthesized:

1. **Energy Efficiency:** You are no longer tired by "being yourself." The friction of the mask is gone.

2. **Ventral Vagal Resilience:** When stress hits, you bounce back to a state of safety and social engagement quickly. You don't get "stuck" in anger or withdrawal.

3. **Congruence:** Your voice tone, your body language, and your words all match. People trust you instinctively because they cannot detect the "micro-tremors" of deception that come from a fragmented self.

If you finish this book and feel a sense of "Settling," a deep exhale in the solar plexus, or a quiet clarity—that is the feeling of your numbers locking into place. It is the sound of the engine finally running on all cylinders.

VI. The Synthesis Protocols: Maintenance for the Future

Synthesis is not a destination; it is a maintenance practice. Entropy affects the soul just as it affects the physical world. Life will try to pull your numbers apart. You will be pressured to wear a mask that doesn't fit (Personality distortion) or to pursue goals that don't feed you (Soul starvation).

To protect your synthesis, adopt these three maintenance protocols:

Protocol 1: The Quarterly Audit

Every 90 days, revisit your core numbers.

- **Check the Fuel:** "Have I fed my Heart's Desire (Vowels) in the last 3 months?" If you are a Soul Urge 5 and haven't traveled, schedule a trip immediately.

- **Check the Vehicle:** "Have I been using my natural talents (Expression)?" If you are an Expression 1 and have been following orders, start a side project where you are the boss.

Protocol 2: The "Shadow" Alarm

Train yourself to recognize your specific "Shadow" behaviors (as identified in Chapter 5) not as failures, but as **System Alarms.**

- If you become aggressive (1 Shadow), it is an alarm that you feel powerless.

- If you become withdrawn (7 Shadow), it is an alarm that you are over-stimulated.

- Do not shame the shadow; decode the alarm and adjust the inputs.

Protocol 3: The Introduction Script

Rewrite the way you introduce yourself to the world to match your synthesized identity.

- **Old Script (Fragmented):** "Hi, I'm [Name], I'm an accountant." (Defining self by the job/Expression).

- **New Script (Synthesized):** "Hi, I'm [Name]. I use financial data (Expression 4) to help families find peace of mind (Heart's Desire 6)."

- This simple linguistic shift signals to your own brain and to others that you are a whole person, not just a function.

VII. Moving Forward: From the Internal to the External

We have now concluded the work of **Book 2**. You have looked in the mirror, taken apart the engine, mapped the dashboard, and signed the peace treaty between your warring factions. You know *who* you are.

But a ship is not built to stay in the harbor. A synthesized identity is meant to encounter the world. Self-knowledge without application is merely "Psychological Entertainment." The purpose of this audit was to prepare you for the collision with reality.

In **Book 3: The External Application**, we will turn our gaze outward.

- We will look at **Time:** How your personal numbers interact with the universal cycles of the years, months, and days. You know *who* you are; soon you will learn *when* to act.

- We will look at **Relationships:** How your synthesized blueprint interacts with the blueprints of lovers, bosses, and children. You will learn the chemistry of compatibility.

- We will look at **Destiny:** The "Pinnacles" and "Challenges" that define the arc of your life story.

You are now ready. The engine is tuned. The map is drawn. The driver is awake.

VIII. The Final Workbook: The Synthesis Declaration

To seal the work of Book 2, complete this final Declaration of Synthesis. Writing this down acts as a psychological anchor for your integrated identity.

Section 1: The Definition

1. **My Internal Engine (Soul Urge):** I am driven by a deep need for

   ____.

2. **My Structural Toolkit (Expression):** I am equipped with the talent of____.

3. **My Social Interface (Personality):** I choose to project an image of

   ____.

Section 2: The Integration

1. **The Bridge:** I will use my talent for [Expression] to satisfy my need for [Soul Urge].

   - *Example: "I will use my talent for Writing (3) to satisfy my need for Wisdom (7)."*

2. **The Protection:** I will use my [Personality] to attract the right people and filter out the noise that distracts my [Life Path].

Section 3: The Vow "I acknowledge that I am a complex system of diverse numbers. I vow to stop suppressing one part of myself to please another. I am the CEO of this internal organization. I accept my contradictions as sources of strength. I move forward into the external world not as a collection of parts, but as a unified whole."

Signed: _________________________________

Date: _________________________________

Reflection Questions: Evaluate Your Authenticity and Self-Image

You have now completed the exhaustive process of the **Internal Audit**. You have mapped the "vocalic breath" of your **Heart's Desire**, the structural "consonant shell" of your **Personality**, and the total "numerical sum" of your **Expression**. You have analyzed the conflicts and drafted an Internal Peace Treaty.

However, in the Pythagorean tradition—and in modern cognitive behavioral science—data without inquiry is inert. To transform this information into lived wisdom, you must move from the *Calculation* stage to the **Self-Reflective** stage. The following chapter is designed to be a "Socratic Probe." These questions are not meant for quick answers; they are designed to trigger what psychologists call **Transformative Learning**—a process that permanently alters your frame of reference.

As you engage with these questions, remember the **Polyvagal** principle: if a question makes your chest tighten or your breath shorten, you have hit a "Friction Point." Do not turn away. That tension is the somatic marker of a hidden truth.

I. The Deep Well: Auditing the Heart's Desire (The Vowels)

The Soul's Hunger and Internal Motivation

The Heart's Desire is the most "private" number in your blueprint. It is the part of you that exists when the lights are off and the phone is silent. It represents your "Autotelic" self—the things you do for no other reason than the joy of doing them.

1. **The Sovereignty of Joy:** Recall a moment in the last year when you felt a sense of "Timelessness" (Flow). You were so engaged that you forgot to eat, check your watch, or perform for others. What was the *mechanical nature* of that activity? If you are a Heart's Desire 3, were you expressing? If a 7, were you analyzing? How does that specific moment of joy validate or challenge your Soul Urge calculation?

2. **The Resentment Map:** Resentment is often a "Soul Alarm" indicating that your Heart's Desire is being starved. Look at the people or situations you resent most right now. Is your resentment rooted in their behavior, or is it rooted in the fact that they are doing what *you* wish you were doing? (e.g., A Soul Urge 5 resenting a "flaky" friend because the 5 is currently over-masking as a rigid 4).

3. **The Starvation Diet:** If your life were a business and your Heart's Desire was the primary shareholder, would that shareholder be satisfied with the current "Dividends" of your daily schedule? If your Soul Urge is 8 (Power/Achievement), but your day is spent in mindless support roles, how much longer can your "Internal Economy" sustain this deficit before a total system collapse (burnout) occurs?

4. **The Secret Altar:** We all have a "Secret Altar"—the thing we value most but are often afraid to admit because of social judgment. A Soul Urge 1 may value absolute independence over family; a Soul Urge 9 may value global causes over personal wealth. Are you currently sacrificing your "Secret Altar" to maintain your "Social Mask"? What would happen if you stopped apologizing for what you actually want?

II. The Toolkit: Auditing the Expression (The Full Name)

Natural Capabilities, Inherited Talents, and Functional Output

Your Expression Number is the "Chassis" of your life. It is the sum total of your capabilities. If the Soul is the *Why*, the Expression is the *How*.

5. **The Functional Efficiency Test:** Efficiency is defined as work output divided by energy input ($E=W/Q$). Look at your professional life. Are you working "hard" (high energy input) but seeing little "output" (W)? This often occurs when you are using the wrong tools. If your Expression is 3 (Creative/Communicative) but you are forcing yourself into a 4 (Structural/Orderly) role, you are operating at 20% efficiency. How much energy are you wasting trying to be "competent" in a frequency that isn't your own?

6. **The Imposter Syndrome Probe:** Imposter syndrome is often a sign that you are successful in a role that belongs to someone else's blueprint. Do you feel like a "fraud" even when you succeed? If so, is it because your success is based on your **Personality Mask** rather than your **Expression Talents**? What would it feel like to be recognized for something that feels "easy" to you?

7. **The Archetypal Alignment:** In **Bloom's Taxonomy**, the highest form of mastery is **Creation**. What is the most significant thing you have "Created" in the last five years? Does this creation look like your Expression Number? (e.g., An Expression 2 creating a harmonious team; an Expression 22 creating a massive infrastructure). If your output doesn't match your toolkit, what is blocking the transmission?

8. **The Capability Gap:** We often ignore our greatest talents because they come so naturally to us that we assume they have no value. "Anyone can do this," we say. But they can't. What is the one thing people always ask you for help with? Does this align with your Expression Number? How can you start charging (literally or figuratively) for this "Natural Frequency"?

III. The Interface: Auditing the Personality (The Consonants)

Public Image, First Impressions, and the Social Mask

The Personality Number is your "User Interface." It is the protective layer.

9. **The Advertisement vs. The Product:** If your Personality Number was a movie poster for your life, what genre would it be? Is it an Action movie (1 or 8), a Documentary (7), or a Romantic Comedy (3 or 6)? Now, look at the "Movie" itself (your Heart's Desire). Is the audience (the public) being misled? Does this "False Advertising" lead to relationships where you feel you have to "perform" to keep people interested?

10. **The Defensive Shell:** When you feel threatened or insecure in a social setting, what is your "Go-To" behavior? Do you become cold and silent (7), aggressive and loud (1), or overly helpful and "people-pleasing" (2/6)? This is your Personality Number in its "Shadow" state. How has this defense mechanism actually prevented you from receiving the support you need?

11. **The First Impression Audit:** Ask three acquaintances (not close friends) what their first impression of you was. Don't defend yourself—just collect the data. Compare their answers to the archetypes in Chapter 3. If they see a "Boss" (8) but you feel like a "Poet" (3), how can you recalibrate your "UI" to be more transparent without losing your protection?

12. **The Aesthetic of the Self:** Look in the mirror. Look at your clothes, your hair, your workspace. Does your physical environment reflect your Personality Number or your Heart's Desire? Synthesis requires that the "Outside" and "Inside" begin to speak the same language. What is one aesthetic change you could make to signal your true frequency to the world?

IV. The Friction Points: Auditing the Synthesis

Conflict Management and the Internal Peace Treaty

This is the most difficult part of the audit. It requires you to look at the "Gears" that are grinding.

13. **The Internal Stalemate:** Identify a major decision you have been procrastinating on. Usually, procrastination is the result of a "Tie Vote" in your internal cabinet. Which part of your blueprint is

voting "Yes" (usually the Soul) and which part is voting "No" (usually the Personality or the pragmatism of the Expression)? What "Bribe" or "Safety Measure" does the "No" vote need to move to a "Yes"?

14. **The Authenticity Gap:** On a scale of 1 to 100, how much of your daily behavior is "Performative" (done to satisfy the expectations of your Personality Mask)? If the number is above 30, you are at risk for **Dorsal Vagal Shutdown** (depression/numbness). What would happen if you lowered that performance by just 10% this week? Who would you disappoint, and why is their approval more valuable than your internal alignment?

15. **The Success Paradox:** Have you ever reached a goal and felt... nothing? This "Anhedonia of Success" occurs when the **Life Path** achieves a milestone that the **Heart's Desire** didn't want. Look back at your greatest "Empty Successes." Which number was driving the car during those times? How can you ensure your next goal is "Soul-Verified"?

16. **The Shadow Signature:** Review the Shadow behaviors of your numbers again. When you are in your Shadow, what is the "Cost of Doing Business"? Who pays the price for your misalignment—your partner, your children, or your own physical health?

V. Somatic Awareness:
The Body as a Blueprint Decoder

Using Polyvagal Theory to Verify Your Numbers

Your body cannot lie. It does not know how to do math, but it knows how to feel frequency.

17. **The Breath Test:** Think about your current career path. Now, take a deep breath. Was it shallow and restricted to the upper chest, or was it deep and expansive? Shallow breathing is the body's way of "Bracing" against a frequency mismatch. If you are a 5 Soul Urge (Freedom) and you think about your 9-to-5 job, does your body "Brace" or "Bloom"?

18. **The Vocal Resonance:** Record yourself speaking about your Heart's Desire. Now record yourself speaking about your daily "Responsibilities." Listen to the pitch and tone. Which one sounds more "Resonant"? According to the **Pythagorean** view, the vowels

in your speech are the windows to your soul. If your voice goes flat when talking about your life, you are "Out of Phase."

19. **The Fatigue Audit:** Not all fatigue is physical. "Numerical Fatigue" is the exhaustion of playing a 4 when you are a 3. Identify the time of day when you feel the most "Drained." What "Number" are you being asked to be at that time? Is it your natural frequency, or an "Applied" frequency?

20. **The Gut-Brain Connection:** We often say we have a "Gut Feeling." In **Polyvagal Theory**, this is the enteric nervous system communicating threat. When you meet people who share your Life Path or Soul Urge numbers, your gut often feels "Warm." When you meet those who are in a "Dissonant" relationship to your numbers, you feel a "Knot." How often have you ignored this "Numerical Neuroception" to your own detriment?

VI. The Legacy Inquiry: Looking Toward Book 3

External Application and the Passage of Time

21. **The Temporal Perspective:** If you were to continue living exactly as you are for the next 9 years (one full Pythagorean cycle), what would the "End Result" be? Would you be a more synthesized version of yourself, or would the "Gaps" in your blueprint be even wider?

22. **The Relationship Mirror:** Look at your closest five relationships. Do these people love your **Personality Mask** or your **Heart's Desire**? If you were to stop "Performing" your Personality Number today, how many of those relationships would survive the transition?

23. **The Contribution Goal:** As we move toward **Book 3**, we will look at how to serve the world. What is the greatest problem in the world that makes you "Angry"? (Anger is often a sign of a blocked 1, 8, or 9 energy). How can your **Expression Number** (Tools) be used to solve that problem while feeding your **Heart's Desire** (Soul)?

24. **The Definition of Success:** Finally, after everything you have learned in Book 2, how has your definition of "Success" changed? Is it still about the destination (Life Path), or is it now about the **Integrity of the Vehicle** (Synthesis)?

VII. Synthesis Practice: The Mirror Dialogue

This is the final, most intensive exercise of Book 2. It requires you to confront yourself in a literal sense.

The Setup: Stand in front of a mirror in a private space. Look directly into your own pupils.

The Script:

1. Address your **Personality Number:** *"I see the mask you wear. I thank you for protecting me, but you are not the master of this house."* (Notice if you feel a sense of relief or fear).

2. Address your **Heart's Desire:** *"I hear what you have been whispering. I am sorry for starving you. From now on, you are the compass."* (Notice if you feel a somatic "opening" in the chest).

3. Address your **Expression:** *"I acknowledge the tools I was given. I stop comparing my vehicle to others. I will use what I have to do what I must."*

4. Address the **Whole:** *"I am [Your Name]. I am a synthesized system. I am no longer a collection of parts. I am in alignment."*

If you can say these things while looking at yourself without flinching, looking away, or feeling like a "liar," you have completed the work of Book 2.

BOOK THREE:
Unlock the Power of Numbers to Transform Your Future

Introduction: Utilize Temporal Cycles for Strategic Planning

Welcome to the third and most pragmatic phase of your journey. In **Book 1**, we identified the "Terrain" of your life through the Life Path—the overarching mission and the permanent geographic features of your destiny. In **Book 2**, we performed a "Forensic Audit" of the vehicle and its driver through the Internal Identity, ensuring that your Soul Urge and Personality were no longer at war. You now possess a profound understanding of who is traveling and where they are going.

However, even the most finely tuned vehicle cannot reach its destination efficiently if it ignores the weather, the tides, and the seasonal shifts of the environment. A Ferrari is the wrong tool for a blizzard; a sailboat is useless in a dead calm.

Book 3 introduces the final, most dynamic dimension of the Pythagorean blueprint: **Time.**

In Western society, we are conditioned to view time as **Linear**—a relentless, one-way conveyor belt moving from a vanished past into an uncertain future. This is the time of "deadlines," "clocks," and "anxiety." It is a framework that suggests time is a finite resource being "spent" until it is gone. However, the Pythagorean tradition, corroborated by modern physics, chronobiology, and macro-economics, views time as **Cyclical.**

From the orbital resonance of planets to the circadian rhythms of your cells, the universe operates in repeating patterns of expansion, consolidation, and release. By the end of this introduction, you will understand how to transition from a "Linear Victim"—constantly surprised by life's changes—to a **"Cyclical Architect,"** utilizing temporal cycles for high-leverage strategic planning.

I. The Great Divergence: Chronos vs. Kairos

To master your future, we must first deconstruct your relationship with the clock. Ancient Greeks utilized two distinct words for time, and the failure to distinguish between them in the modern age is the primary cause of systemic burnout and strategic failure.

1. Chronos: The Quantitative Measure

Chronos is the root of "chronology." It is time as a measurable resource—minutes, hours, days. It is the "Horizontal" axis of existence. In the world of *Chronos,* every hour is treated as identical to the next. A Monday in the dead of winter is mathematically identical to a Friday in the height of summer. The corporate world operates almost exclusively in *Chronos,* demanding a flat line of peak productivity 365 days a year. This is biologically and mathematically impossible, leading to the "friction" of the modern soul.

2. Kairos: The Qualitative Opportunity

Kairos is the "Vertical" axis. It refers to the "Opportune Moment" or the "Season." It is the realization that not all moments are created equal. There is a "right time" to plant and a "right time" to harvest. In the realm of *Kairos,* an hour spent in a **1 Personal Year** (Initiation) might yield ten times the results of an hour spent in an **8 Personal Year** (Material Harvest) if the goal is to start a new business.

The Strategic Shift: Most people live entirely in *Chronos.* They attempt to start businesses, end marriages, or launch investments based on external pressure or arbitrary calendar dates. They try to "force" a harvest in the middle of a winter cycle. Book 3 is your manual for *Kairos.* It teaches you to identify the specific "Numerical Season" you are in so you can stop swimming against the tide and start utilizing the natural momentum of your specific cycle.

II. The Biological Imperative: Periodicity and the Human System

Our insistence on linear time is actually a biological and psychological hallucination. Our bodies are entirely cyclical; we are rhythmic beings living in a rhythmic universe. Within your system, thousands of "clocks" are ticking simultaneously, governed by the law of **Periodicity.**

- **Circadian Rhythms:** Your 24-hour sleep/wake cycle, regulating cortisol and melatonin.

- **Ultradian Rhythms:** Shorter cycles of energy and focus occurring every 90-120 minutes.

- **Infradian Rhythms:** Cycles longer than a day, such as the lunar cycle, seasonal affective shifts, and reproductive cycles.

When you ignore these biological rhythms—staying up all night or eating at erratic hours—your health fails. Similarly, when you ignore your **Numerical Rhythms,** your destiny "stutters." You experience "bad luck," which is often just a code word for "bad timing."

Numerology is effectively the **Macro-Biology of the Soul.** Just as your body knows when to sleep to recover, your Personal Year cycle knows when your career needs to "sleep" (a **7-Year**) so that it can be reborn with explosive energy in the next cycle (a **1-Year**). Strategic planning is simply the act of aligning your *Chronos* (your calendar) with your *Kairos* (your numerical season).

III. The Law of the Nine: Understanding the Epicycle

The core of Pythagorean temporal forecasting is the **9-Year Epicycle.** In base-10 mathematics, 9 is the final single digit—the limit of a specific density of information before it rolls over into a new octave (10, which reduces back to 1).

Life does not move in perfect circles; it moves in **Spirals.** You never return to the exact same place, but you do return to the same *frequency* at a higher level of maturity. If you did not learn the lesson of "Independence" during your last 1-Year cycle nine years ago, the universe will present the same lesson again, though the stakes will be higher.

The Fractal Seasons of the 9-Year Cycle

To utilize these cycles for planning, you must view the nine years as a fractal of a single growing season:

- **Year 1: The Emergence (Spring Equinox).** The ego is reborn. This is a high-voltage year for planting seeds. The soil is fresh, and the energy is unmatched. If you do not initiate here, you have nothing to harvest in Year 8.

- **Year 2: The Germination (Moisture).** A year of waiting, partnership, and extreme patience. The seeds are underground. If you dig them up to check for progress, you kill them. You must nurture and cooperate.

- **Year 3: The First Bloom (Expansion).** Socialization, creativity, and self-expression. The plant breaks the surface. This is a year for "marketing" your ideas and making connections.

- **Year 4: The Pruning (Rooting).** Hard work, structure, and meticulous detail. This is the "Foundation Year." If the roots aren't set deeply here, the plant will topple in the upcoming 5-Year storm.

- **Year 5: The Cross-Pollination (Change).** Mid-cycle disruption. Freedom, travel, and unexpected shifts. This year tests the strength of your Year 4 foundation.

- **Year 6: The Flowering (Responsibility).** Duty, home, family, and community. The plant is now part of the ecosystem. It is a year for adjusting the "vessels" of your life.

- **Year 7: The Photosynthesis (Introspection).** A year of silence and study. The plant isn't growing outward; it is processing light into energy. Attempting to "hustle" in a 7-Year is like trying to force a flower to bloom in a dark room.

- **Year 8: The Harvest (Power).** The manifestation of everything started in Year 1. This is the year of "Results," "Money," and "Authority." It is the peak of the mountain.

- **Year 9: The Decomposition (Composting).** The year of endings. Letting go of what no longer serves you to fertilize the soil for the next Year 1.

IV. The Architecture of the Future:
Four Layers of Forecasting

In the chapters to follow, we will build your 5-year strategic plan using four distinct layers of forecasting. To understand the future, you must understand how these layers "stack" upon one another, creating a complex weather system for your soul.

Layer 1: The Life Pinnacles (The Climate)

Pinnacles are long-term cycles lasting between 9 and 27 years. If the Personal Year is the "weather," the Pinnacle is the **Climate**. If you are in a "Tropical" pinnacle, even your "Winter" years will be relatively productive. If you are in a "Desert" pinnacle, your "Spring" years will require much more irrigation. We will calculate your four major life pinnacles in **Chapter 2**.

Layer 2: The Personal Year (The Season)

This is the primary focus of **Chapter 1**. It dictates the overarching theme of your current 365-day period. Understanding this prevents "Temporal Friction"—the act of trying to force an outcome that the current season does not support.

Layer 3: Monthly and Daily Cycles (The Weather)

This is tactical timing. Just as a sailor checks the daily wind, we use Monthly and Daily cycles to pick the specific "Kairos" for signing contracts, launching products, or initiating difficult conversations. We use the formula: Personal Month = Personal Year + Calendar Month.

Layer 4: The Universal Year (The Global Current)

Every year, the world itself has a collective number (e.g., 2026 is a **1 Universal Year**; $2+0+2+6=10 \rightarrow 1$). We will learn how to "calculate the delta"—the difference between your personal frequency and the world's frequency. When your 1-Year aligns with a 1-Universal Year, the power of initiation is doubled.

V. From Reactive to Proactive: The Mastery of Ends

The most profound benefit of Book 3 is learning the **Mastery of the 9-Year Cycle**. Most people are terrified of endings. They cling to dying jobs, toxic relationships, and outdated self-images because they view an "End" as a failure. This resistance creates the majority of human suffering.

- **The Reactive Life:** You are fired or dumped unexpectedly in a 9-Year. You feel like a victim of "bad luck." You scramble to replace the loss immediately, often repeating the same mistake because you didn't take the time to clear the soil.

- **The Proactive Life:** You recognize you are entering a **9 Personal Year**. You know the "Composting" phase has begun. You spend the year voluntarily "pruning" your life. You finish old projects. You say your goodbyes to habits that have expired. When the "End" comes, it isn't a tragedy; it's a graduation. You are already standing at the door of the new cycle, unencumbered by the past.

Chapter 1: Forecast Your Personal Year and Monthly Cycles

Now that you understand the overarching philosophy of **Kairos**—the recognition of qualitative time over mere quantitative duration—it is time to perform the actual calculations that will define your immediate future. In the previous chapters, we established that time is not a flat, linear desert, but a series of rhythmic, rising, and falling waves. To navigate these waves, you must move from abstract theory to the concrete mathematics of your personal timeline.

By the end of this section, you will be able to pinpoint exactly where you are located within your current 9-year epicycle. More importantly, you will learn to navigate the specific "weather" of the coming months and days. This is the difference between an amateur sailor who is constantly surprised by a storm and a master navigator who reads the barometer and adjusts the sails before the first drop of rain falls.

I. Calculating the Personal Year: The Macro-Vibration

Your **Personal Year** is the overarching theme, the "Grand Narrative," that governs your life from January 1st to December 31st of any given year. While some modern numerologists debate whether the year begins on your actual birthday or the calendar New Year, the Pythagorean school and the systems-theory approach emphasize the **Universal Year transition** as the primary shift in global frequency.

Think of the Universal Year as the "Atmospheric Pressure" of the entire planet. When the calendar flips, the global vibration shifts, and that shift filtered through your personal birth data creates your unique Personal Year.

The Formula for Temporal Alignment

To find your Personal Year, you sum the digits of your **Month of Birth**, your **Day of Birth**, and the **Current Universal Year** you are inquiring about.

Personal Year = Birth Month + Birth Day + Universal Year

Example Calculation:

Let us assume you were born on **October 12th** and you wish to find your vibration for the year **2026**.

1. **Reduce the Birth Month:** October is the 10th month. $1 + 0 = 1$.
2. **Reduce the Birth Day:** 12th day. $1 + 2 = 3$.
3. **Reduce the Universal Year:** 2026. $2 + 0 + 2 + 6 = 10$. Then $1 + 0 = 1$.
4. **Sum the Components:** 1 (Month) + 3 (Day) + 1 (Year) = 5

Result: In 2026, you are in a **5 Personal Year.**

This number 5 is your "Vibrational Mandate" for the next twelve months. It is the frequency that will color every opportunity, challenge, and internal mood you encounter.

II. The Nine Archetypal Years: A Comprehensive Strategic Guide

Once you have determined your number, you must stop resisting its inherent nature. Strategic failure occurs when an individual attempts to execute a "Year 8" strategy (Aggressive expansion) during a "Year 7" cycle (Introspective study). Below is the high-definition breakdown of each year's potential.

Year 1: The Emergence (Spring Equinox)

- **Theme:** New beginnings, planting, seeds, and self-assertion.
- **Strategic Action:** This is the most critical year of the nine. It is the time to launch new businesses, sign new contracts, and reinvent your physical appearance.
- **The Shadow:** Procrastination. If you do not act in Year 1, you will have no harvest in Year 8.

Year 2: The Germination (Moisture and Patience)

- **Theme:** Partnership, diplomacy, waiting, and detail.
- **Strategic Action:** The seeds are underground. You cannot see progress, so you must network and build alliances. It is a year of "The Other."
- **The Shadow:** Aggression. Forcing a seed to grow by pulling on the stem only kills the plant.

Year 3: The First Bloom (Social Expansion)

- **Theme:** Creativity, communication, joy, and social mobility.
- **Strategic Action:** This is your "Marketing Year." Give speeches, write your book, and expand your social circle.
- **The Shadow:** Scattering energy. Don't let the social whirl prevent you from finishing what you started.

Year 4: The Pruning (The Foundation)

- **Theme:** Hard work, structure, order, and physical health.
- **Strategic Action:** Organize your taxes, fix your house, and commit to a rigid health regime.
- **The Shadow:** Laziness or cutting corners. A weak foundation leads to a collapse in Year 5.

Year 5: The Cross-Pollination (The Pivot)

- **Theme:** Change, freedom, travel, and uncertainty.
- **Strategic Action:** Expect the unexpected. Pivot your career, travel, and embrace chaos.
- **The Shadow:** Recklessness. Change for the sake of change can lead to instability.

Year 6: The Flowering (Responsibility)

- **Theme:** Duty, home, service, and domestic harmony.
- **Strategic Action:** Focus on family and community. Renovate your home or your relationships.
- **The Shadow:** Martyrdom. Do not lose your identity in others' burdens.

Year 7: The Photosynthesis (The Sage)

- **Theme:** Introspection, analysis, study, and silence.
- **Strategic Action:** This is a "Sabbatical Year." Seek wisdom over material expansion.
- **The Shadow:** Materialistic greed. Forcing money matters here usually leads to loss.

Year 8: The Harvest (Material Power)

- **Theme:** Manifestation, finance, authority, and karma.
- **Strategic Action:** Step into leadership. Ask for the promotion. Manage your investments.
- **The Shadow:** Abuse of power. What you sowed in Year 1 returns to you now.

Year 9: The Decomposition (Completion)

- **Theme:** Endings, pruning, forgiveness, and release.
- **Strategic Action:** Clean house. End toxic relationships. Do not start major new ventures.
- **The Shadow:** Clinging to the past. Resistance to endings causes immense pain here.

III. Zooming In: The Tactical Calculus of Months and Days

While the Personal Year provides the "Climate," the **Personal Month** provides the "Forecast." In professional strategic planning, the Year is your 5-year goal; the Month is your quarterly target. This is where you make high-leverage tactical decisions.

The Personal Month Formula

The month number is always dependent on the year you are in.

Personal Month = Personal Year + Calendar Month

> **Example:** You are in a **5 Personal Year** and it is **March (the 3rd month).**
>
> 5 (Year) + 3 (Month) = 8.
>
> Your month of March has an **8 vibration.**

Even though your *year* is about change and chaos (5), your *month* of March is about money and power (8). This is the "Kairos" window! If you need to sign a lease or negotiate a salary during your chaotic 5-year, you do it in March.

The Personal Day Formula: The "Micro-Vibration"

For the most precise timing—such as choosing a wedding date or a surgery—we calculate the **Personal Day.**

Personal Day = Personal Month + Calendar Day

> **Example:** It is **March 15th** in the example above.
>
> 1.   March is an **8 Personal Month.**
> 2.   The day is **15.** 1 + 5 = 6.
> 3.   Calculation: 8 + 6 = 14. Then 1 + 4 = 5.
>
> **Result:** Your Personal Day is a **5.** This indicates a day of movement and high-speed communication.

IV. The "Numerical Delta": Aligning with the Universal Current

Strategic mastery requires understanding the "Delta"—the difference between your personal cycle and the collective cycle of the world.

2026 is a 1 Universal Year (2+0+2+6=10 → 1). The entire world is currently in a state of "Seed Planting."

- **The Harmonic Alignment:** If you are in a **1 Personal Year**, your frequency matches the world. You have a "Tailwind."

- **The Dissonant Delta:** If you are in a **9 Personal Year** during this **1 Universal Year**, you will feel internal-external tension. The world is screaming "Go!" while your soul is screaming "Wait!"

If you ignore your "9" and try to follow the world's "1," you will build the new venture on un-cleared, toxic soil.

V. Workbook: Your Personal Temporal Forecast

Complete the following sections to map your current and upcoming cycles. Do not proceed until you have verified your math.

Part A: The Macro-Audit (Your Personal Year)

1. **My Birth Month (Reduced):** _______
2. **My Birth Day (Reduced):** _______
3. **Current Universal Year (2026 = 1):** _______
4. **Sum (1 + 2 + 3):** _______
5. **My Personal Year Number:** _______ (This is your "Climate").

Part B: The Tactical Forecast (The Next 3 Months)

Using the formula: Personal Year + Calendar Month = Personal Month

Month	Personal Year	+	Calendar Month	=	Personal Month	Strategic Intent
January		+	1	=		
February		+	2	=		
March		+	3	=		

Part C: Analyzing the Delta

1. Is your Personal Year higher or lower than the Universal Year (1)?

   ____

2. If your number is higher (e.g., 9), where are you feeling the pressure to "hurry up" when you need to "slow down"? _________

   ____

3. List one major goal for this year: _________________________________

4. Does this goal match the "Strategic Action" of your year number?
    If not, how can you pivot the goal to match the frequency?

    ____

    ____________________________147________________________

    ____

Chapter 2: Prepare for Major Life Pinnacles and Challenges

If the Personal Year cycles discussed in the previous chapter represent the "Daily Weather" and the "Four Seasons," then the **Life Pinnacles** represent the "Climatic Eras" of your existence. In the geography of your destiny, a Personal Year 1 might be a sunny day, but if that day occurs during an "Ice Age" Pinnacle, the temperature will remain significantly lower than if it occurred during a "Tropical" Pinnacle.

To master your future, you must understand the long-form architecture of your life. Most people operate with a short-term bias, focusing on the next twelve months. However, the Pythagorean system reveals that your life is divided into **four distinct developmental phases**, each governed by a specific number that dictates your overarching requirements for success, your environmental conditions, and your primary psychological lessons.

By the end of this chapter, you will have calculated your four Life Pinnacles, identified your "Life Challenges," and developed a strategic roadmap for the decades ahead.

I. The Anatomy of a Pinnacle:
The Four Seasons of a Lifetime

A Pinnacle is a specific period of time during which you are presented with certain opportunities and environmental conditions. It is as if the universe has given you a specific "Assignment" for a period of roughly nine to twenty-seven years.

There are four Pinnacles in every life:

1. **The First Pinnacle (The Spring):** This covers your "Formative Years," generally from birth until somewhere between the ages of 27 and 35. It is the era of learning, family influence, and finding your initial footing.

2. **The Second Pinnacle (The Summer):** A nine-year period covering your early-to-mid career and the establishment of your own family or independent creative output.

3. **The Third Pinnacle (The Autumn):** Another nine-year period covering mid-life. This is often the peak of your influence and material contribution.

4. **The Fourth Pinnacle (The Winter):** This covers the remainder of your life. It is the era of legacy, wisdom, and spiritual synthesis.

II. The Calculus of Destiny:
Calculating Your Pinnacle Numbers

The math for Pinnacles is derived directly from your **Birth Date**. Unlike the Personal Year, which changes annually, these numbers are baked into your blueprint from the moment of your arrival.

The Formulas

- **Pinnacle 1 (Birth Month + Birth Day):** This represents the energy of your youth.

- **Pinnacle 2 (Birth Day + Birth Year):** This represents the energy of your early adulthood.

- **Pinnacle 3 (Pinnacle 1 + Pinnacle 2):** This represents your mid-life "harvest."

- **Pinnacle 4 (Birth Month + Birth Year):** This represents your late-life legacy.

- **Important Note:** Always reduce each component (Month, Day, Year) to a single digit **before** adding them together, unless they are Master Numbers (11 or 22), which stay as they are.

Example Calculation:

Let's use a birth date of **October 12, 1990.**

- **Month:** 10 (1 + 0 = 1)
- **Day:** 12 (1 + 2 = 3)
- **Year:** 1990 (1 + 9 + 9 + 0 = 19 → 1 + 9 = 10 → 1)

1. **Pinnacle 1:** Month (1) + Day (3) = 4
2. **Pinnacle 2:** Day (3) + Year (1) = 4
3. **Pinnacle 3:** P1 (4) + P2 (4) = 8
4. **Pinnacle 4:** Month (1) + Year (1) = 2

III. The Timing Table: When Do Your Pinnacles Shift?

The shift from the First Pinnacle to the Second is determined by your **Life Path Number.** Because the 9-year cycle is the heartbeat of the system, we subtract your Life Path from the number 36 (a multiple of 9) to find the "Turning Point."

Life Path	End of 1st Pinnacle	End of 2nd Pinnacle	End of 3rd Pinnacle	4th Pinnacle Starts
1	Age 35	Age 44	Age 53	Age 54+
2	Age 34	Age 43	Age 52	Age 53+
3	Age 33	Age 42	Age 51	Age 52+
4	Age 32	Age 41	Age 50	Age 51+
5	Age 31	Age 40	Age 49	Age 50+
6	Age 30	Age 39	Age 48	Age 49+
7	Age 29	Age 38	Age 47	Age 48+

Life Path	End of 1st Pinnacle	End of 2nd Pinnacle	End of 3rd Pinnacle	4th Pinnacle Starts
8	Age 28	Age 37	Age 46	Age 47+
9	Age 27	Age 36	Age 45	Age 46+

IV. Interpreting Your Pinnacle Numbers: The Environmental Mandates

Once you have your numbers, you must look at them as "Job Descriptions" for that phase of your life. If you ignore the mandate of your current Pinnacle, you will feel like you are walking through waist-deep water.

Pinnacle 1: Individuality and Leadership

In this era, you are forced to stand on your own feet. If this occurs in your youth (1st Pinnacle), you may have felt isolated or pushed into early responsibility. In later life, it demands that you innovate and lead.

Pinnacle 2: Cooperation and Sensitivity

This era demands diplomacy and partnership. You are learning to work with others. If you try to be an "Alpha" during a 2 Pinnacle, you will meet constant resistance. This is a time for detail, patience, and waiting.

Pinnacle 3: Self-Expression and Social Influence

A highly creative and social era. This Pinnacle is about the "Joy of Life." You will find success through communication, writing, art, or social networking. The danger here is scattered energy and lack of depth.

Pinnacle 4: Structure, Work, and Hardship

A "Building" era. This is not a time for "get rich quick" schemes. You are required to work hard, organize your life, and build a lasting foundation. It can feel restrictive, but it produces the most solid results.

Pinnacle 5: Freedom, Change, and Expansion

The most unpredictable Pinnacle. Expect frequent moves, career shifts, and travel. You are learning to be flexible. If you try to hold on to security too tightly, the 5-energy will "shake" it out of your hands.

Pinnacle 6: Responsibility, Home, and Duty

The "Nurturing" era. Success comes through domestic harmony, community service, and caring for others. It is often a time of marriage, raising children, or caring for elderly parents.

Pinnacle 7: Analysis, Wisdom, and Specialization

A quiet, introspective era. You are not meant to focus on material gain but on spiritual or technical mastery. This is the era of the "Scholar" or the "Specialist."

Pinnacle 8: Material Power and Manifestation

The era of big business, finance, and large-scale leadership. You are tested on your ability to handle power. If you have been ethical, the rewards are immense. If not, the losses are equally large.

Pinnacle 9: Universal Love and Completion

An era of high idealism. You are learning to let go of personal desire for the benefit of humanity. It is a time of broad influence and spiritual "graduation."

V. The Life Challenges: Your Internal Friction Points

While Pinnacles describe the *external* environment, **Challenges** describe your *internal* psychological hurdles. These are the "Shadows" you must master to unlock the power of your Pinnacles.

The Challenge Formulas:

- **Challenge 1:** Birth Month - Birth Day
- **Challenge 2:** Birth Day - Birth Yea
- **Challenge 3 (The Main Challenge):** Challenge 1 - Challenge 2
- **Challenge 4:** Birth Month - Birth Year

Note: Challenge 3 is the "Great Barrier" that often persists through your entire middle life.

Interpreting the 0 Challenge:

If your calculation results in a 0, you are a "Free Agent." You have all the challenges available to you, or none at all. It indicates a life where you have significant choice in your development, but it requires extreme self-discipline to stay on track.

Interpreting the 4 Challenge:

A 4 Challenge indicates a struggle with discipline and order. You may feel like a "slacker" or, conversely, be so rigid that you break. Success requires you to embrace the "Grind" without resentment.

VI. Workbook: Mapping Your Long-Term Roadmap

Do not skip this section. Write your results here.

Your Birth Data:

Birth Month (Reduced): ______________________________________

Birth Day (Reduced): ______________________________________

Birth Year (Reduced): ______________________________________

1. Calculate Your Pinnacles:

- P1 (Month + Day): ______________________________________

- P2 (Day + Year): ______________________________________

- P3 (P1 + P2): ______________________________________

- P4 (Month + Year): ______________________________________

2. Identify Your Turning Points (Use the Table in Section III):

- My Life Path: ______________________________________

- Age of 1st Shift: ______________________________________

- Age of 2nd Shift: ______________________________________

- Age of 3rd Shift: ______________________________________

3. Identify Your Main Challenge (Challenge 3): ____________________

VII. Strategic Planning for Pinnacle Shifts

Shift years (the ages listed in your table) are often the most turbulent times of your life. During these years, your "Numerical Climate" is changing.

The Transition Protocol:

1. **The Two-Year Window:** You will begin feeling a Pinnacle shift roughly two years before it actually occurs. If you are moving from a 4 (Work) to a 3 (Social), you will start feeling an "itching" boredom with your routine.

2. **Inventory Check:** What "Tools" worked in your last Pinnacle that will no longer work in the next? (e.g., If moving from a 1 to a 2, your aggressive "Solo" approach must be traded for diplomacy).

3. **The Challenge Audit:** How is your "Main Challenge" currently sabotaging your Pinnacle goals?

Chapter 3: Improve Interpersonal Connections via Numerical Compatibility

In Books 1 and 2, we treated your life as a laboratory for the self. We analyzed your internal mechanics—the hidden engines of your Soul Urge and the outward transmission of your Expression. We scrutinized your personal timeline to understand how your history shaped your current trajectory. But as any architect knows, a building does not stand alone; it exists within a neighborhood, susceptible to the shadows of taller towers and the structural integrity of the ground it shares with others.

No human being exists in a vacuum. We are social animals, and our success—both material and emotional—is largely determined by the quality of our relationships. Whether it is the person you wake up next to, the business partner you sign contracts with, or the family members who hold your history, these connections are the "Relational Interface" of your life.

Most relationship advice focuses on communication styles, "love languages," or psychological attachment theories. While valuable, these are often symptoms rather than causes. Pythagorean numerology reveals something deeper and more primal: **Vibrational Physics.** In this chapter, we move beyond the "Solo Blueprint" to explore the mechanics of how human frequencies interlock. You will learn why you feel an instant, inexplicable "spark" with certain individuals (Resonance), why others seem to drain your psychic battery (Dissonance), and how to navigate the inevitable "Friction Points" in any partnership using the **Compatibility Matrix.**

I. The Physics of Connection: Resonance vs. Dissonance

Everything in the universe, at its most fundamental level, is a frequency. From the spin of an electron to the orbit of a galaxy, vibration is the language of existence. When two human frequencies meet—represented by their numerical blueprints—one of three distinct mathematical phenomena occurs. Understanding these is the key to moving from "hoping" for a good relationship to "architecting" one.

1. Resonance: Constructive Interference

In physics, resonance occurs when two objects vibrate at the same natural frequency, causing the amplitude of the vibration to increase. In human terms, this is the "soulmate" or "perfect partner" feeling. It is **Constructive Interference**: your strengths amplify theirs, and their presence makes your life feel "louder" and clearer. You finish each other's sentences not just because of familiarity, but because your "Roads" (Life Paths) are vibrating in the same key.

2. Dissonance: Destructive Interference

Dissonance occurs when frequencies clash, creating a "beat frequency" that manifests as static, tension, or a "jagged" energy. This is the relationship where, despite immense love or shared history, you are constantly arguing over trivialities. Your vibrations are "out of phase." One person is pushing when the other is pulling. This creates **Destructive Interference**, where the energy of the relationship actually subtracts from the energy of the individuals.

3. Neutrality: Different Octaves

Many people in your life—colleagues, acquaintances, or distant relatives—exist in a state of neutrality. Your frequencies occupy different octaves or different "rooms" of the numerical house. You do not clash, but you also do not amplify. These are the people who pass through your life without leaving a lasting mark on your structural integrity.

The Core Realization: Compatibility is not a moral judgment. A "bad" match doesn't mean the other person is "bad"; it means your frequencies are mathematically dissonant. In **Predictive Architecture**, we stop trying to "fix" the person and start "tuning" the connection.

II. The Core Compatibility Calculation: The Synastry Map

To truly analyze a relationship, looking at a single number is insufficient. You must create a **Synastry Map**—a comparative overlay of the three core numbers of both individuals. This reveals where the relationship is strong and where it is vulnerable to collapse.

The Three Levels of Connection

Just as a house has a foundation, a plumbing system, and a facade, a relationship has three distinct layers of interaction:

1. **Life Path Compatibility (The Road):** This is the "Macro-Connection." Can you build a life together? Do your long-term goals align? If one person is on a Life Path 1 (pioneering/solitary) and the other is on a Life Path 2 (cooperative/dependent), the "Roads" are moving at different speeds. Without awareness, one will feel dragged while the other feels held back.

2. **Heart's Desire Compatibility (The Bedroom & The Hearth):** This is the "Internal Connection." This governs what you want emotionally and what makes you feel safe. It represents your "Fuel." If your Heart's Desires match, you can survive a lot of external friction because your souls are speaking the same language. If they clash, the relationship will feel "empty" even if you are successful in the world.

3. **Personality Compatibility (The Kitchen & The Social Circle):** This is the "Micro-Connection." It governs day-to-day habits, social behavior, and first impressions. Dissonance here leads to "The Bickering Couple"—people who love each other deeply (Heart's Desire match) but can't agree on how to load the dishwasher or what to wear to a party.

The Relationship Vibration Formula

Beyond the individual numbers, the relationship itself creates a "Third Energy"—an entity that exists between the two people.

Person A (LP) + Person B (LP) = Relationship Number

- **Example:** A Life Path 1 (Independent) and a Life Path 6 (Nurturing) create a **7 Relationship**. This bond will naturally gravitate toward mystery, privacy, and intellectual or spiritual pursuits. It may feel "cool" or "detached" to outsiders, but for the couple, it is a shared sanctuary of study and depth.

III. The Archetypal Pairings:
Natural, Compatible, and Challenging

Pythagorean theory organizes the numbers 1 through 9 into three distinct "Triads." Numbers within the same triad speak the same "dialect" of energy.

1. The 1-5-7 Triad: The Intellectuals and Visionaries

These are the "Mind" numbers. They value independence, mental stimulation, and personal space above all else.

- **Best For:** Innovative business partnerships, long-distance relationships, or couples who both value having a "room of one's own."

- **The Dynamics:** They respect each other's need for autonomy.

- **The Risk:** A lack of emotional "glue." If two 7s get together, they may become so private and introspective that they stop communicating entirely, becoming "two ships passing in the night."

2. The 2-4-8 Triad: The Builders and Pragmatists

These are the "Body" numbers. They value security, financial stability, and tangible results.

- **Best For:** Traditional marriages, large-scale business ventures, and the complex logistics of raising a family.

- **The Dynamics:** They are highly efficient. One manages the details (2 or 4) while the other handles the executive power (8).

- **The Risk:** "The Spreadsheet Trap." They can become so focused on building the empire that they forget to inhabit it. The relationship can become a business transaction.

3. The 3-6-9 Triad: The Creatives and Humanitarians

These are the "Soul" numbers. They value emotion, artistic expression, and "The Greater Good."

- **Best For:** Artistic collaborations, passionate romantic bonds, and nonprofit/activist work.

- **The Dynamics:** They are warm, expressive, and deeply connected to the human experience.

- **The Risk:** "The Drama Vortex." These numbers feel everything intensely. Without a "Building" number (4 or 8) to ground them, they can spin out into emotional volatility or financial instability.

IV. Navigating Dissonant Pairings: The Bridge Number

What happens when you fall in love with your "Numerical Opposite"? For example, a Life Path 1 (The Rugged Individualist) and a Life Path 2 (The Sensitive Diplomat). In many systems, this is labeled a "bad match." In **Predictive Architecture**, there are no bad matches—only **unmanaged frictions.**

To bridge the gap between dissonant frequencies, we use the **Bridge Number.** This is the mathematical middle ground that represents the "common language" both people must learn to speak to avoid structural collapse.

The Bridge Formula

Person A - Person B = Bridge Number

- **The 1 and 2 Bridge (1):** To survive, the 2 must give the 1 absolute autonomy and leadership in specific areas. The 1, in turn, must use their strength to "protect" the 2's sensitivity. The "Bridge" is independence; if they become too enmeshed, the 1 will feel suffocated and the 2 will feel bullied.

- **The 4 and 5 Bridge (1):** The 4 wants structure; the 5 wants chaos. This is one of the most difficult pairings. The Bridge of 1 suggests that they must maintain a "First-Person" focus—pursuing their own separate interests so that they don't try to "fix" the other's frequency.

V. Business Compatibility:
Building the "Mastermind" Team

Numerical compatibility is perhaps most vital in the professional sphere, where emotional sentiment cannot hide structural inefficiency. To build a "Mastermind" team, you do not want a collection of identical numbers. You want a **Full Spectrum Symphony**.

The Mastermind Roles:

1. **The Visionary (1 or 5):** Provides the "Year 1" energy. They see the gap in the market. They are the pioneers.

2. **The Architect (4 or 22):** Turns the vision into a blueprint. Without a 4, the 1's vision remains a dream that never materializes.

3. **The Producer (8):** The person who understands power and money. They "Manifest" the 4's blueprint into the material world.

4. **The Spokesperson (3):** The 3 can "sell" anything. They translate the technical work of the 4 into a social frequency that people want to buy.

5. **The Glue (2 or 6):** Every team needs a "Harmonizer." They detect the subtle frictions between the high-power 1s and 8s and resolve them before the system breaks.

The "Danger Zone":

- **Too many 8s:** A constant, exhausting power struggle for the "CEO" chair.

- **Too many 7s:** "Analysis Paralysis." The team will have perfect data and zero sales.

- **Too many 3s:** Incredible brainstorm sessions, but no one ever takes notes or follows through on the logistics.

VI. The Temporal Connection:
The Moving Target of Love

This is the most advanced—and often most overlooked—aspect of compatibility. Relationships are not static; they are dynamic systems moving through time. Even "Natural Pairings" can experience crisis if their **Personal Year Cycles** become dissonant.

The "Seven-Year Itch" Explained

In numerology, the "Seven-Year Itch" is often actually a **Cycle Dissonance**.

- **Scenario:** You are in a **Personal Year 9** (Completion/Letting Go). You feel an internal need to "prune" your life, quit your job, or withdraw into silence.

- **Conflict:** Your partner is in a **Personal Year 1** (New Beginnings/Aggression). They want to buy a house, start a family, and move fast.

The partner in the 1-Year feels the partner in the 9-Year is "depressed" or "unsupportive." The partner in the 9-Year feels the partner in the 1-Year is "insensitive" or "manic." **Neither is wrong.** They are simply in different seasons.

Strategic Action for Temporal Harmony:

- **Support the Season:** If your partner is in a **Personal Year 4** (Hard Work/Foundation), do not plan a surprise "adventure" vacation (a 5-Year activity). It will stress them out. Instead, offer to help them with their taxes or take over the household chores so they can focus on their "4-Year" grind.

- **Acknowledge the Gap:** Simply stating, "I know you are in a year of beginnings and I am in a year of endings," can de-escalate 90% of relational tension. It moves the conflict from "You are doing this to me" to "Our cycles are currently out of sync."

VII. Workbook: Mapping Your Relationship Matrix

Select one significant person in your life—a partner, a business associate, or a family member—and perform this Forensic Relational Audit.

Subject Name: ____

Step 1: The Core Overlay

- **My Life Path:** ____

- **Their Life Path:** ______________________________________

- **Relationship Triad:** Are you in the same Triad (1-5-7, 2-4-8, or 3-6-9)? ____

  (If yes, you share a common "operating system." If no, you must learn their "language.")

Step 2: The Third Energy

- **Relationship Number (My LP + Their LP):** _________________
  - *Interpretation:* * **1-3:** A relationship of high activity and social output.
    - **4-6:** A relationship of duty, home building, and security.
    - **7-9:** A relationship of deep spiritual or intellectual mystery.

Step 3: Finding the Bridge

- **The Bridge Number (|My LP - Their LP|):** _________________
  - *Look up this number in Book 1. This is the quality you both must cultivate to keep the peace.*

Step 4: The Temporal Delta

- **My Personal Year:** _________________________________
- **Their Personal Year:** _______________________________
- **The Gap:** Are your years "Harmonic" (e.g., 1 and 3, or 2 and 4) or "Conflicting" (e.g., 4 and 5, or 7 and 8)? _________________

Chapter 4: Select Ideal Dates for Important Life Events

In the preceding chapters, we identified the broad "Climatic Eras" of your life through the **Pinnacles** and the "Seasonal Shifts" of your years via **Personal Year cycles.** You now possess the map of the terrain and the forecast for the weather. However, for the **Predictive Architect**, knowledge of the season is only half the battle. If Book 1 was about the destination and Book 2 was about the vehicle, Book 3—and specifically this chapter—is about the **Launch Window.**

The final level of mastery in the Pythagorean blueprint lies in **Tactical Timing:** the surgical ability to select the exact day, hour, and minute to initiate high-stakes actions. In the Pythagorean tradition, this is known as the study of **Electional Numerology.** It is the art of choosing a "Birth Date" for an entity that is not biological—a marriage, a corporation, a legal contract, or a real estate acquisition.

Just as your biological birth date bestowed upon you a Life Path that dictates your natural talents and hurdles, the date you sign a deed or launch an app gives that entity its own "Numerical DNA." By the end of this chapter, you will transition from a reactive participant in time to a proactive **Chronographic Engineer,** utilizing the Numerical Calendar to choose the perfect **Kairos** for your most important life events.

I. The Theory of the "Second Birth"

Every significant event has a "Natal Chart." In the realm of quantum physics and systems theory, the initial conditions of any system largely determine its long-term trajectory. This is often referred to as "Sensitive Dependence on Initial Conditions." In Numerology, we call this the **Second Birth**.

When you incorporate a company, the moment the paperwork is legally stamped is the "Birth" of that legal person. When you stand at an altar and say "I do," that moment is the "Birth" of the marriage. These entities do not have souls in the human sense, but they possess **Vibrational Momentum**.

The Blueprint of the Event

If you launch a business on a **4 Universal Day** (the vibration of structure, persistence, and limitation), that business will naturally require immense manual labor, rigid organization, and meticulous accounting to survive. It may be highly stable, but it will never feel "easy." Conversely, if you launch that same business on a **3 Universal Day** (expression, expansion, and socialization), the business will thrive on marketing, word-of-mouth, and creative energy.

The goal of Tactical Timing is to align the **Nature of the Event** with the **Vibration of the Day**. Misalignment creates "Temporal Drag." You would not want to launch a fun, creative party-planning business on a day that vibrates to the number **7** (Solitude, Analysis, and Secrecy), as the energy of the day would constantly pull the business toward niche specialization and away from the social spotlight. Similarly, you would never want to perform a complex, delicate medical surgery on a day that vibrates to the number **5** (Chaos, Change, and Sudden Shifts).

II. Calculating the "Event Vibration"

To select a date with architectural precision, we must look at the intersection of two distinct forces: the Global Current and the Individual Alignment.

1. The Universal Day (The Global Current)

The Universal Day is the frequency of the world at large. It is the "atmospheric pressure" affecting everyone on the planet simultaneously. It is obtained by summing the Month, Day, and Year of any given calendar date and reducing it to a single digit (or a Master Number).

Universal Day = Month + Day + Year

> **Example:** You want to launch a website on **March 15, 2026**.

- o **Month:** March is 3.
- o **Day:** 15 reduces to 6 (1 + 5 = 6).
- o **Year:** 2026 reduces to 1 (2 + 0 + 2 + 6 = 10 1).
- o **Calculation:** 3 + 6 + 1 = 10 → 1.
- o **Result:** This is a **1 Universal Day**—the absolute best vibration for a "New Beginning" or an initial launch.

2. The Personal Day (The Individual Alignment)

As we established in Chapter 1, your Personal Day is the specific "Kairos" window for *you*. It is how the global current filters through your unique energy field. Even if the world is in a high-energy **1 Universal Day**, if your **Personal Day is a 9**, you will feel an internal "drag." You might feel tired, reflective, or prone to ending things rather than starting them.

The most successful events—the ones that feel "blessed" or "lucky"— occur when the **Universal Day** and the **Personal Day** are in **Harmonic Resonance**. For a major launch, you ideally want both numbers to be active (1, 3, 5, or 8).

III. The Strategic Calendar: What to Do and When

The following table serves as your master blueprint for electional timing. Choosing a date that matches your intent is the equivalent of a sailor waiting for a favorable wind.

Intent of Event	Ideal Universal Day	The Numerical Logic
New Business Launch	**1 or 8**	**1** provides the spark of initiation; **8** provides the vibration of material success and efficient management.
Weddings & Engagements	**2, 6, or 9**	**2** for partnership; **6** for domestic harmony and responsibility; **9** for the highest form of universal compassion.

Intent of Event	Ideal Universal Day	The Numerical Logic
Signing Contracts / Deeds	**4** or **8**	**4** ensures the contract is legally "heavy" and binding; **8** ensures the exchange is profitable for all parties.
Parties & Social Events	**3** or **5**	**3** encourages communication and laughter; **5** brings a sense of excitement, surprise, and adventure.
Travel & Relocation	**5**	The number of movement. It minimizes delays and encourages new perspectives during the journey.
Research & Surgery	**7**	The vibration of the specialist. It encourages focus, deep analysis, and technical perfection.
Debt Repayment / Closures	**9**	The frequency of completion. It ensures the "karmic loop" is closed and will not return.

IV. Avoiding the "Collision Dates"

Just as there are "Green Light" days, there are "Red Light" days where the vibration of the day diametrically opposes the intent of the event. We call these **Collision Dates.**

1. The 5 Collision: The Disruption Factor

Never schedule a highly structured, detail-oriented, or traditional event on a **5 Universal Day.** The frequency of 5 is "Disruption" and "Freedom." If you schedule a traditional wedding on a 5 Day, expect the flowers to be wrong, the officiant to be late, or a sudden thunderstorm to move the ceremony. The 5 energy hates "The Plan."

2. The 4 Collision: The Lead Weight

Avoid launching a creative, "free-spirited," or fast-moving project (like a viral marketing campaign) on a **4 Universal Day.** The energy of 4 is "Heavy" and "Earth-bound." It is excellent for pouring concrete or doing taxes, but for a creative launch, it will make the project feel mired in bureaucracy and endless "re-dos."

3. The 1-9 Conflict: The False Start

The most common mistake is starting a new venture on a **Personal Day 9**. Because the Universal Year might be a 1, you feel the external pressure to move. However, your internal 9-cycle is busy "composting" the past. Starting a business here is like planting a seed in soil that hasn't been cleared of weeds. You will likely lose all passion for the project within nine months.

V. The Hour of Power: Refining the Timing

For the elite strategist, the Day is only the "Macro" level. To truly engineer a moment, we can refine the timing down to the **Personal Hour**. The Pythagorean system utilizes a 24-hour cycle where each hour carries a sub-frequency that colors the day's main vibration.

The Hourly Formula:

Personal Hour = Personal Day + Current Hour (Military Time)

Practical Application:

Imagine your **Personal Day is an 8** (Power/Money). You have a crucial meeting to sign a contract. You want the *hour* to support "Structure."

- If you meet at **2:00 PM** (14:00 in military time):
- 8 (Day) + 14 (1+4=5) = 13 → 4.
- **Result: A 4 Personal Hour.** This is a "Power Hour" for a contract because it adds a layer of "4-Foundation" to your "8-Material Success." The deal is more likely to be long-lasting and legally sound.

Conversely, if you met at **3:00 PM** (15:00):

- 8 + 15 (1+5=6) = 14 → 5.
- **Result: A 5 Personal Hour.** This would be a "High-Risk Hour." The meeting might be interrupted, or the terms might suddenly shift.

VI. Deep Dive Case Studies:
The Anatomy of Success and Failure

To understand the weight of Tactical Timing, we must look at how these vibrations manifest in real-world scenarios.

Case A: The "Accidental" Bankruptcy

A tech startup launched their app on a **Universal Day 9**. Their intention was global reach and "changing the world" (vibrations associated with 9). However, they ignored the fact that 9 is the vibration of **The End**. While the launch was celebrated, the company struggled with "retention" from day one. Users would join and then immediately leave (The 9-Exit). Within eighteen months—two 9-month cycles—the company folded. They had "born" the company into a cycle of completion rather than initiation.

Case B: The Harmonic Wedding

A couple—a **Life Path 3** (The Communicator) and a **Life Path 6** (The Nurturer)—sought an ideal wedding date. They initially looked at a Saturday that fell on a **Universal Day 5**.

- **Analysis:** A 5 Day would have been chaotic for a 6-Life Path bride who values order and home.

- **The Correction:** They moved the wedding to a Sunday, which reduced to a **Universal Day 6**.

- **Result:** The event was described by guests as the most "harmonious and welcoming" ceremony they had ever attended. The marriage was "born" into the vibration of the Home and Family (6), aligning perfectly with the bride's Life Path.

VII. Advanced Electional Strategy: The 5-Day "Buffer"

When selecting a date for a major event—like a product launch or a house closing—never look at the date in isolation. Look for a **Cluster of Resonance.**

1. **The Lead-Up:** Ensure the three days *prior* to your launch are not 9-Days. You want the momentum to be building (1, 2, 3) not dissolving.

2. **The Launch:** The "Day of the Deed" should match the intent.

3. **The Anchor:** The day *after* the launch should ideally be a **4 or 8 Day**. This "anchors" the new energy into the physical world, ensuring it doesn't just flare up and disappear like a 5-vibration spark.

VIII. Workbook: Planning Your Next Big Move

This section is designed to help you apply the "Hour of Power" and "Universal Current" to a real-life goal. Think of one major event you have coming up (a move, a job application, a major purchase, or a difficult conversation).

The Event Objective: _______________________________________

(e.g., "Sign the lease on the new office with favorable terms.")

Step 1: The Personal Day Audit

Calculate your Personal Day for your preferred date.

- My Personal Year: _______________________________________
- Calendar Month: _______________________________________
- Calendar Day: _______________________________________
- **My Personal Day:** _______________________________________

Step 2: The Universal Day Audit

Calculate the Universal Day for the same date.

- Month + Day + Year: _______________________________________
- **Universal Day:** _______________________________________

Step 3: The Alignment Check

Does the **Universal Day** match the **Intent** (Refer to the table in Section III)?

- [ ] Yes
- [ ] No (If no, consider moving the date by +/- 1 day to find a better frequency).

Step 4: The Hour of Power Selection

Using your **Personal Day,** find a time that creates a "Harmonic Hour."

- Target Personal Hour: _______________________________________
- Military Time to meet: _______________________________________

Chapter 5: Construct a Five-Year Plan Based on Personal Cycles

In the previous chapters, we have dismantled the machinery of time. You have learned to identify the high-altitude "Eras" of your life (**Pinnacles**), the seasonal "Weather" of your years (**Personal Years**), and the tactical "Windows" of your days (**Personal Days**). However, the ultimate goal of the **Predictive Architect** is not merely to survive the next twenty-four hours or even the next twelve months. The goal is **Legacy**.

Strategic dominance requires a medium-to-long-range horizon. Without a multi-year blueprint, you remain a reactive entity—sailing beautifully, perhaps, but without a definitive port of call. In this 3,500-word chapter, we will synthesize everything you have learned into a **Five-Year Numerical Strategic Plan**. We will map your personal frequencies against the upcoming global shifts, allowing you to build a fortress of stability and expansion that spans half a decade. This is where we transition from understanding time to **owning it.**

I. The Philosophy of the Quinquennium

The five-year plan, or *quinquennium*, is a staple of Roman administration and modern corporate strategy for a reason: it is the shortest span of time in which a radical transformation of "Self" and "Estate" can occur. In Numerology, five years represents more than half of a full 9-year epicycle. This means that within any five-year window, you will experience:

1. **At least one major "Tipping Point":** A shift from an internal/reflective phase (Years 2, 7, 9) to an external/manifestation phase (Years 1, 3, 5, 8).

2. **A "Foundation" year:** A period where you are required to secure your assets (Year 4).

3. **A "Pivot" year:** A period of radical change or disruption (Year 5).

By mapping these in advance, you move from "hope" to "engineering." You stop asking "What will happen to me?" and start asking "What will I build with the energy provided?" Most people fail because they try to force a Year-8 harvest in a Year-4 pruning season. By viewing your life in five-year blocks, you develop the **Strategic Patience** required to wait for your window and the **Aggressive Intent** to strike when it arrives.

II. The Five-Year Projection Matrix

To build your plan, we must first lay out the numerical "Climate" for the next five years. We will use the year **2026** as our Year 1 starting point—a year that is globally significant as it marks the beginning of a new **Universal 1 Cycle.**

Step 1: Calculate Your Personal Year Sequence

Using the formula from Chapter 1 (Birth Month + Birth Day + Universal Year), calculate your Personal Year for 2026 through 2030.

Example (October 12 birth):

- **2026 (Universal 1):** Personal Year 5 (Change/Travel)
- **2027 (Universal 2):** Personal Year 6 (Responsibility/Home)
- **2028 (Universal 3):** Personal Year 7 (Analysis/Spirit)
- **2029 (Universal 4):** Personal Year 8 (Harvest/Power)
- **2030 (Universal 5):** Personal Year 9 (Completion/Release)

Step 2: Identify the "Universal Delta"

Every year has a **Universal Year** vibration. Your strategy must account for the "Delta"—the difference between your personal internal push and the world's external pull.

Year	Universal Number	Global Theme	Your Strategic Posture
2026	1	Global Initiation	High competition. New Tech. Market entry.
2027	2	Global Diplomacy	Alliances. Consolidation. Slow-down.
2028	3	Global Expression	Social expansion. Creative "bubbles." Inflation.
2029	4	Global Consolidation	Infrastructure. Regulation. Hard limits.
2030	5	Global Disruption	Freedom movements. Pivots. Volatility.

III. Strategic Objectives: The 9-Year Arc

Once your sequence is mapped, you must assign **Strategic Objectives** to each year based on its vibration. A five-year plan that tries to "hustle" every year is doomed to burnout and failure. A numerical plan includes "Strategic Rest" and "Structural Maintenance."

The Years of Initiation (1, 3, 5, 8): The "Go" Phase

These are your years of maximum external output. In your five-year plan, these are the dates you set for product launches, property purchases, and career pivots.

- **Year 1:** The Seed. (New identity, new company).
- **Year 3:** The Bloom. (Marketing, public speaking, social networking).
- **Year 5:** The Pivot. (Expansion, travel, diversification).

- **Year 8:** The Harvest. (Capitalizing on gains, leadership, high-finance).

The Years of Consolidation (2, 4, 6): The "Protect" Phase

These are your years of fortification. If you spend these years trying to start new things, you will find the world resists you. Instead, use these for:

- **Year 2:** The Bridge. (Networking, subtle influence, waiting).

- **Year 4:** The Wall. (Taxes, legal structures, health optimization, saving money).

- **Year 6:** The Hearth. (Family, community, service, home renovation).

The Years of Interiority (7, 9): The "Audit" Phase

These are the years where you "clean the cache." They are vital for long-term health.

- **Year 7:** The Library. (Specialized education, meditation, spiritual retreat).

- **Year 9:** The Pruning. (Ending toxic contracts, forgiveness, letting go).

IV. Designing the "Pivot Point": The Year 5 Strategy

The most dangerous part of a five-year plan is the **Year 5 shift.** In our example above, the individual enters a Personal Year 5 in 2026. This means their *entire* five-year plan is "born" into a vibration of change.

If your 5-Year Plan contains a **Personal Year 5**, you must build **Antifragility** into your strategy. A Year 5 is like a hurricane; you don't fight it, you build a structure that can sway without breaking.

- **Tactical Action: The "Optionality" Principle.** Do not sign 10-year leases in a Year 5. Opt for flexible contracts and remote-capable infrastructures.

- **Tactical Action: Liquid Reserves.** Keep a higher percentage of liquid capital (20–30% more than usual). The Year 5 vibration often presents "Flash Opportunities"—sudden chances to buy an asset or join a venture—that require immediate cash and zero hesitation.

V. The Master Schedule: 2026 - 2030

To provide a concrete example of a **Numerical Strategic Plan**, we will map out a hypothetical individual who is moving from a **Personal Year 1 (2026)** to a **Personal Year 5 (2030)**.

Year 1 (2026): The Individual Mandate (Universal 1 / Personal 1)

- **Theme:** Double Intensity.
- **Action:** This is a "Once-in-a-Generation" launch window. Start the primary project of your life. Take extreme risks. Focus purely on self-interest and personal branding.
- **Objective:** Establish a new revenue stream.

Year 2 (2027): The Alliance Mandate (Universal 2 / Personal 2)

- **Theme:** Harmonized Support.
- **Action:** The world is slowing down, and so are you. Seek partners. Focus on the "Back-end" of the business. Do not try to lead every meeting; learn to listen.
- **Objective:** Sign three major joint-venture agreements.

Year 3 (2028): The Expression Mandate (Universal 3 / Personal 3)

- **Theme:** Social Explosion.
- **Action:** High creative output. This is the year to write your book or launch your podcast. Your charm is at its peak.
- **Objective:** Increase brand visibility by 400%.

Year 4 (2029): The Structural Mandate (Universal 4 / Personal 4)

- **Theme:** Grounded Foundations.
- **Action:** The most difficult year of the five. Stop expanding. Organize your bookkeeping. Invest in your physical body (preventative health). Buy real estate if possible.
- **Objective:** Eliminate all high-interest debt and secure legal trademarks.

Year 5 (2030): The Expansion Mandate (Universal 5 / Personal 5)

- **Theme:** Collective and Personal Freedom.
- **Action:** Pivot. If the world is shifting, shift with it. Travel to new markets. This is the year to diversify your portfolio.
- **Objective:** Launch a secondary, global product line.

VI. Managing the "Delta" Stress

The core difficulty in a five-year plan is when your Personal Year and the Universal Year are in **Opposition**. For instance, if you are in a **Personal Year 4** (Hard work/Saving) while the world is in a **Universal 3** (Socializing/Spending).

- **The Stressor:** You feel like you are missing the party. The world is out dancing and spending money, while you are at home doing your taxes and building a foundation.

- **The Strategic Fix:** Recognize that your "4" foundation will protect you when the world's "3" bubble eventually pops. Stick to your personal numbers over the global hype.

Strategic mastery is the ability to ignore the "FOMO" (Fear Of Missing Out) generated by the Universal Year and stay true to your Personal Year mandate.

VII. Workbook: Your Five-Year Architectural Blueprint

Fill this out based on your specific birthday and current Life Path. Use a pencil; as a Predictive Architect, you must remain precise but adaptable.

1. The Projection Matrix

Calculate your Personal Year (PY) for the next five years using the formula: Birth Month + Birth Day + Universal Year.

- 2026 (Universal 1): PY ______
- 2027 (Universal 2): PY ______
- 2028 (Universal 3): PY ______
- 2029 (Universal 4): PY ______
- 2030 (Universal 5): PY ______

2. The High-Leverage Year (The Pinnacle)

Identify which year in your 5-year block is a **Personal Year 8** or **Personal Year 1**.

- **Target Year:** ____
- **Specific Goal:** ____
- *Note: This is the anchor of your entire plan. Everything else is either preparation or cleanup for this year.*

3. The "Silent" Year (The Inventory)

Identify your **Personal Year 7** or **Personal Year 9**.

- **Target Year:** ____
- **Scheduled "Pullback":** _______________________________________
- *Note: What will you stop doing during this year to save your energy for the harvest?*

4. The Health and Wealth Foundation

Identify your **Personal Year 4** or **Personal Year 6**.

- **Target Year:** ____
- **Structural Focus:** ____
- *Note: Will you focus on home renovation, paying off a mortgage, or a physical health overhaul?*

Conclusion: Standardize the Practice of Forecasting in Your Life

We have traveled from the abstract geometry of the Pythagorean vacuum to the concrete realities of your five-year strategic blueprint. You have transformed from a spectator of time—someone to whom things simply "happen"—into a **Predictive Architect**. You now possess the specialized vocabulary of the universe: the cycles, the pinnacles, and the vibrational deltas that dictate the rise and fall of human endeavor.

However, the greatest risk to any architect is not a lack of knowledge, but the failure to maintain the structure once it is built. A blueprint is a static document; life is a kinetic experience. To truly master the **Kairos** (the opportune moment) of your existence, you must move beyond the periodic study of these numbers and into a state of **Standardized Practice**. This conclusion serves as your manual for integrating numerical forecasting into your daily, monthly, and yearly operating rhythm.

I. The Shift from Intuition to Calculation

Most people navigate their lives using a combination of "gut feeling," cultural conditioning, and reactive emotion. While intuition is a powerful tool, it is often clouded by biological stress, hormonal shifts, and external social pressure. When you feel an urge to quit your job, is it because your soul is ready for a new beginning (a Personal Year 1), or is it simply because you are exhausted in the middle of a structural grind (a Personal Year 4)?

By standardizing the practice of forecasting, you provide your intuition with a mathematical guardrail. You learn to distinguish between a "passing mood" and a "vibrational mandate." Intuition tells you *that* something is changing; Numerology tells you *why* and *when.*

Consider the "Practitioner's Oath" as the foundational code of your new lifestyle: **I will not make major life-altering decisions based on temporary emotional states without first consulting the numerical weather of my current cycle.** This isn't about ignoring your feelings; it is about contextualizing them. It is the difference between a sailor who fears every wave and the navigator who understands the tides.

II. The Daily Ritual: The Micro-Forecast

The most successful users of this system do not wait for a crisis to check their numbers. They integrate a 30-second audit into their morning routine. Just as you check the weather to decide whether to carry an umbrella, you check your Personal Day to decide how to carry yourself.

The Standard Operating Procedure (SOP) for Your Day:

1. **Calculate the Personal Day:** Personal Month + Calendar Day
2. **Set the Tactical Intent:** * **1 Day:** Be decisive; initiate the conversation you've been avoiding.

    o **2 Day:** Listen more than you speak; seek harmony and collaboration.

    o **3 Day:** Prioritize social expansion and creative expression.

    o **4 Day:** Focus on the "boring" details; clean your desk; fix the leaks.

    o **5 Day:** Expect the unexpected; be flexible with your schedule.

    o **6 Day:** Focus on service, family, and domestic responsibilities.

    o **7 Day:** Withdraw; prioritize deep work and analysis over meetings.

    o **8 Day:** Make the "Ask"; focus on money, power, and manifestation.

    o **9 Day:** Let go; finish the task; clear the psychic clutter.

3. **Review the "Hour of Power":** If you have a high-stakes meeting, use the formula

Personal Day + Military Hour

to find the most harmonic 60-minute window for that specific task.

III. The Monthly Review: The Tactical Pivot

At the end of every calendar month, the global vibration shifts. This is your opportunity to zoom out from the daily "static" and look at the "Quarterly" movement of your life. Standardizing this practice involves a **Monthly Audit** where you compare your actual results with the numerical forecast.

The Delta Analysis

Did you struggle with a project this month? Check if you were trying to execute a "9-energy" (ending) task during a "1-energy" (beginning) month. Often, our frustration isn't born from a lack of talent, but from a mismatch of timing. Use the end of the month to "re-tune" your instruments.

Resource Allocation

Look ahead to the next month's number. If the next month is a **Personal Month 8**, start preparing your financial documents and sales pitches now. Don't let the "Harvest Month" catch you with empty barns. If the next month is a **7**, clear your social calendar so you can dive deep into study or research without the guilt of saying "no" to friends later.

IV. The Yearly Sabbatical: The Macro-Audit

Once a year—ideally during the transition of the Universal Year (January 1st) or on your Birthday—you must perform a deep-tissue audit of your Pinnacles and Challenges.

Life is not a flat line; it is a spiral. Every year you return to the same calendar months, but you are at a different height on the spiral because your Personal Year has shifted. Standardizing this involves:

- **Reviewing the Pinnacle:** Are you nearing the end of a 9-year era? If so, the "9-Year Itch" is not a sign that something is wrong, but a sign that you are outgrowing your current container.

- **Updating the 5-Year Plan:** As established in Chapter 5, your five-year plan is a living document. Every year, you add a new year to the horizon and refine the "Pivot Points" based on the wisdom you gained in the previous twelve months.

V. Ethics of the Architect: Forecasting for Others

As you become proficient in reading the "weather" of time, you will inevitably begin to calculate the numbers for your partner, your children, and your colleagues. This brings a profound ethical responsibility. The goal of forecasting for others is **Compassion, Not Control.**

The goal of forecasting for others is not to manipulate them, but to develop radical empathy. When you realize your spouse is in a **Personal Year 9**, you stop taking their withdrawal personally. You realize they are in a state of "Composting," and your role is to provide the space for that release. When you see your employee is in a **Personal Year 4**, you recognize that their sudden focus on detail is a vibrational gift to the company, not a sign of being "difficult."

Forecasting allows you to see the "hidden weather" others are walking through. It turns judgment into support.

VI. The "Numerical Hygiene" of the Home and Office

Standardization extends beyond the mind and into the physical environment. Your home and office are the "Charging Stations" for your energy. They should reflect the cycle you are currently inhabiting.

For the 4-Foundation Practitioner

Keep your physical space meticulously organized during "Building" years. Chaos on your desk leads to chaos in your 4-cycle. Use these years to invest in heavy furniture, filing systems, and structural repairs.

For the 5-Expansion Practitioner

During your 5-year pivots, introduce movement into your space. Change the furniture, open the windows, and ensure your environment reflects the "Air" and "Freedom" of the 5-vibration. If you are stuck in a rigid environment during a 5-cycle, you will feel a mounting sense of claustrophobia.

VII. Navigating the Dissonance: When the Math Doesn't "Feel" Right

There will be times when your Personal Day is an **8** (Power/Money), but you feel like a **2** (Sensitive/Emotional). This is known as **Vibrational Friction.**

Standardizing your practice means trusting the math over the mood. If the day is an 8, the "Current" of the world is moving toward material manifestation. Even if you feel "low," if you take action, you will find that the universe supports you more than usual. The numbers are the **Wind**; your mood is the **Tide**. You can sail against the tide if you have the wind at your back. Successful architects do not wait for the "perfect mood" to build; they follow the schedule set by the blueprint.

VIII. The Predictive Architect in a Global Context

As we move toward the end of this decade, the **Universal Year Cycles** will become increasingly volatile. We are moving toward a period where the global "Personal Year 1" (2026) will demand a total rewrite of our social and economic contracts.

By standardizing your forecasting practice, you become a "Node of Stability" in a chaotic system. While others are panicked by sudden market shifts or social upheavals, you will see them as the inevitable "Pivot Points" (Year 5) or "Consolidations" (Year 4) of a larger global entity. You will not just survive these shifts; you will anticipate them. You will move your capital, your family, and your energy *before* the storm hits, not during it.

IX. Workbook: The Standardization Checklist

Commit to the following integration steps to ensure your architectural mastery remains permanent.

1. The "Morning Briefing" Integration

Where will you record your daily number? (e.g., A physical journal, a digital calendar, or a dedicated app?)

____

____

____

____

2. The "Relational Map"

Who are the three people whose cycles you will track alongside your own to improve your empathy and communication?

____

____

____

____

3. The "Yearly Review" Date

Mark the date you will perform your annual Five-Year Plan update.

____

____

____

____

4. The Physical Audit

What one change will you make to your workspace this week to align with your current **Personal Year**?

____

____

____

____

Reflection Questions: Review Your Readiness for Future Cycles

The blueprint is finalized. The tactical calendar is set. The strategic five-year horizon is mapped. You have transitioned from a passive observer of time to an active architect of your own destiny. But before you step through the threshold of this book and back into the kinetic world of 2026, you must undergo a "Structural Integrity Test."

In the world of architecture, a building must be inspected before it is occupied. In the world of **Predictive Architecture**, that inspection takes the form of deep, numerical self-reflection. These questions are not mere exercises; they are the final calibration of your internal instruments. They are designed to expose the "weak points" in your current understanding and reinforce the "load-bearing walls" of your future strategy.

Spend significant time with each section. Do not rush the calculation of your answers. The clarity you find here will determine whether your next Personal Year is a triumph of engineering or a collapse into old patterns.

I. The Personal Year Audit:
Aligning with the Current Tide

Understanding the theory of a Personal Year is simple; living in alignment with its frequency is a discipline. These questions test your ability to distinguish your ego's desires from the vibrational mandate of your current cycle.

1. **The Seasonal Match:** Looking back at the last three months, can you identify three specific instances where you resisted the "Weather" of your Personal Year? (e.g., You tried to force a new beginning in a Year 9, or you tried to hide away in a Year 3). What was the energetic cost of that resistance?

2. **The Resource Check:** If you are in a **Years 4 or 7**, have you allocated sufficient "Time Equity" for maintenance and study? If you are in a **Years 1 or 8**, do you have the "Energy Capital" required to sustain a high-output launch?

3. **The Shadow Frequency:** Every number has a shadow. If you are in a **Year 5**, are you using "freedom" as an excuse for "avoidance"? If you are in a **Year 6**, is your "service" actually "martyrdom"? How will you correct this imbalance in the coming quarter?

II. The Relational Interface:
Testing Your Social Physics

As established in Chapter 3, you are not a solo tower; you are part of a relational neighborhood. These questions review your ability to manage the "Vibrational Physics" between yourself and others.

4. **The Dissonance Audit:** Identify the person in your life who currently causes you the most "Static." Calculate their current Personal Year. How much of your conflict is a clash of character, and how much is simply a **Temporal Mismatch** (e.g., You are in a Year 1 "Go" and they are in a Year 4 "Slow")?

5. **The Bridge Number Application:** For your most important partnership, what is your **Bridge Number**? Have you actively practiced that specific trait this month? If not, what is one concrete action you can take tomorrow to "cross the bridge"?

6. **The Mastermind Team:** Look at your professional circle. Are you missing a specific frequency? Do you have too many "Visionaries" (1s and 5s) and not enough "Builders" (4s and 8s)? Who do you

need to recruit into your circle to complete the "Full Spectrum Team"?

III. Tactical Timing:
Reviewing the Electional Windows

The mastery of the "Hour of Power" and the "Universal Day" separates the amateur from the architect. These questions assess your readiness to implement Tactical Timing in real-world scenarios.

7. **The Launch Review:** Think of a major project that failed to gain momentum in the past. If you calculate the **Universal Day** of its launch now, does the vibration match the intent? What would you do differently if you were launching that project today?

8. **The "Hour of Power" Habit:** Do you have a recurring high-stakes event (e.g., a weekly sales call or a monthly board meeting)? How can you shift the start time of this event by 30 or 60 minutes to align with a more harmonic **Personal Hour**?

9. **The Collision Date Awareness:** Look at the next 30 days of your calendar. Do you have any "Structure-Heavy" tasks scheduled on **Universal 5 Days**? How will you build "Disruption Insurance" into those days to account for the chaotic frequency?

IV. The Five-Year Horizon:
Assessing the Long-Range Blueprint

Strategy is the art of sacrifice. To say "yes" to a Year-8 Harvest, you must say "no" to a thousand distractions in the years prior.

10. **The Year-8 Target:** Is your current lifestyle building the "infrastructure" required for your next **Personal Year 8**? If that year arrived tomorrow, would you have the assets ready to harvest, or would you be scrambling to plant the seeds?

11. **The Pivot Readiness:** If 2030 (a **Universal 5 Year**) brings a radical shift in your industry, is your current Five-Year Plan "Antifragile"? Do you have multiple revenue streams or skills that can pivot into a new frequency?

12. **The "Emptying" Phase:** Most people fear the **Personal Year 9**. Are you psychologically prepared to let go of a project, a habit, or a relationship that no longer fits your 5-year blueprint, even if it feels "safe" right now?

V. Standardization and Integration: The Final Inspection

The value of this book is zero if the knowledge remains between its covers. This final section tests your commitment to the **Standardized Practice** of forecasting.

13. **The Daily Ritual:** Where is the friction in your morning routine? What is preventing you from spending 30 seconds calculating your **Personal Day**? How will you remove that friction (e.g., putting a sticky note on your coffee maker or an alert on your phone)?

14. **The Intuition vs. Math Balance:** Can you recall a moment where your "gut" told you to go, but the "numbers" said wait? Which one did you follow, and what was the outcome? How will you use the **Practitioner's Oath** to navigate similar conflicts in the future?

15. **The Legacy Question:** If you follow this blueprint perfectly for the next five years, what will be the "Life Path" of your legacy? What will you have built that stands independently of your daily effort?

VI. The Architect's Final Calibration Table

Use the table below to do a final "Hard Audit" of your readiness for 2026 and beyond.

Domain	Readiness Score (1-10)	Primary Weak Point	One Corrective Action
Self-Alignment			
Relational Physics			
Tactical Timing			

Domain	Readiness Score (1-10)	Primary Weak Point	One Corrective Action
Long-Range Strategy			
Daily Integration			

VII. A Closing Benediction for the Predictive Architect

You have finished the study. Now begins the work.

The numbers of the Pythagorean system are not your prison; they are your playground. They are the scaffolding upon which you will hang the beauty, the effort, and the love of your life. As you step out into the "Universal 1" of 2026, remember that the most successful buildings are those that respect the laws of physics while reaching for the sky.

Respect the cycles. Honor the timing. Build for the long term.

The universe is counting on you.

Overall Conclusion: Integrate Numbers into a Cohesive Lifestyle

You stand now at the summit of a mountain of data. Behind you lies the valley of the "Unexamined Life," where time was a confusing, linear march and events seemed to strike with the random cruelty of a lightning bolt. Before you lies the open landscape of the **Predictive Architect**. We have moved through the structural anatomy of your soul (Book 1), the rhythmic seasons of your journey (Book 2), and finally, the tactical engineering of your days and years (Book 3).

This conclusion is not a summary; it is an **Integration Protocol**. The ultimate failure of most practitioners is compartmentalization—using Numerology only when things go wrong, or treating it as a hobby rather than a high-level cognitive framework. To achieve true mastery, you must move beyond "using" numbers and begin **inhabiting** them. This chapter will show you how to standardize your practice, harmonize your environment, and evolve into a person for whom the future is a collaborator rather than a mystery.

I. The Transmutation of Time: From Chronos to Kairos

To integrate numbers into a cohesive lifestyle, you must first change your fundamental relationship with time. The Western world is obsessed with **Chronos**—the quantitative, ticking clock that measures time in equal, indifferent segments. Chronos is the tyrant of the "Deadline" and the "Efficiency Metric."

The Predictive Architect works with **Kairos**—the qualitative, opportune moment. Kairos is the "Right Time" that cannot be measured by a standard watch.

- A **Personal Year 1** is a Kairos for starting, regardless of what the Gregorian calendar says in January.

- A **Personal Hour 7** is a Kairos for silence, even if your Chronos-clock says it's time for a loud networking lunch.

Integration means learning to ignore the artificial pressure of Chronos when it conflicts with the vibrational truth of Kairos. When you standardize this, you no longer feel "behind" in life. You realize that you cannot be "late" to a cycle that hasn't arrived yet, and you cannot "miss" a window that you have architecturally prepared for.

II. The Standardized Operating Procedure (SOP) of the Architect

A lifestyle is simply the sum of your repetitions. If you want a "Cohesive Lifestyle," you must build a daily, weekly, and monthly cadence that feels as natural as breathing.

1. The 60-Second Morning Alignment

Every morning, before you open your email or engage with the digital "noise" of the world, perform the **Numerical Triage**.

- **Identify the Universal Day:** What is the "Current" of the world today?

- **Identify the Personal Day:** How does that current affect me specifically?

- **Identify the Challenge:** Look at the day's number—what is the shadow? (e.g., If it's a 5 Day, the challenge is scattered focus).

- **Set the Anchor:** Choose one task that perfectly matches the day's vibration. If it's a 4 Day, make that task "Organize the 2026 Tax Folder."

2. The Sunday "Cycle Sync"

Every Sunday evening, look at the upcoming seven days.

- **Map the "Clash Points":** Do you have a big presentation on a Personal Day 7? (A clash between the need for solitude and the need for performance).
- **Schedule the "Hour of Power":** Adjust your high-stakes meetings by 15 or 30 minutes to land in a harmonic Personal Hour.

3. The Quarterly "Pinnacle Check"

Every three months, zoom out. Review your **Pinnacles**. Are you acting in accordance with the long-range era you are in? If you are in a Pinnacle of 3 (Creativity/Joy), but you have spent the last quarter doing nothing but 4-energy accounting, you are creating a "Vibrational Debt" that will eventually manifest as burnout.

III. Numerical Feng Shui: Harmonizing Your Physical Space

Integration is not just mental; it is environmental. Your physical surroundings should serve as a "Reinforcement Loop" for your current cycles.

- **The Year 4/Foundation Office:** If you are in a Personal Year 4, your office should be a fortress of order. Use heavy materials, dark woods, and filing systems that symbolize "The Wall."
- **The Year 3/Creative Studio:** If you are in a Personal Year 3, introduce bright colors, open spaces, and tools for expression.
- **The Personal Year 9 "Clearance":** As you approach a Year 9, your home should undergo a radical purging. If you hold onto physical clutter during a 9-cycle, you are literally "blocking the drain" of your next 9-year epicycle.

IV. The Social Contract: Managing the "Others"

One of the most profound shifts in a cohesive lifestyle is how you interact with the people around you. You must move from **Judgment to Attunement**.

When you know the Life Paths and Personal Years of your inner circle, your "Social Physics" changes:

- **Parenting:** You stop trying to force a "Life Path 7" child (the loner/thinker) to be a "Life Path 3" social butterfly. You align your parenting style with their numerical DNA.

- **Leadership:** In your business, you stop assigning "Year 7" employees (who need deep focus) to "Year 5" projects (which require constant travel and disruption). You become a "Human Resource Architect" who places people where their current cycle provides the most momentum.

V. Financial Architecture: Timing the Market of Life

A cohesive lifestyle requires financial peace. Numerology provides the "Investment Calendar" that traditional advisors often miss.

- **Personal Year 8 (The Harvest):** This is the year to sell, to ask for the raise, and to maximize your liquid assets.

- **Personal Year 4 (The Foundation):** This is the year to buy the land, to set up the trust, and to focus on "Low-Risk, Long-Term" stability.

- **Universal Year 1 (2026):** As the world resets, look for "Blue Ocean" opportunities. This is not a year for following trends; it is a year for setting them.

VI. The Ethics of Prediction: Power and Humility

As you conclude this book, you possess a level of foresight that most people would find supernatural. With this power comes the **Architect's Responsibility.**

1. **Do Not Use Numbers to Bypass Effort:** Numerology shows you the wind, but you still have to sail the boat. An "8-Year" will not bring you money if you stay in bed.

2. **Respect the Agency of Others:** Never use someone's numbers to manipulate them. Use the data to *serve* the relationship, not to control it.

3. **The Law of Compensation:** For every "Harvest" you take in an 8-Year, you must "Plant" in a 1-Year and "Compost" in a 9-Year. The lifestyle is circular, not linear.

VII. Integrating the "Master Numbers" into Daily Life

If you carry 11, 22, or 33 in your chart, your "Lifestyle Integration" requires an extra layer of discipline. You are navigating a "High-Voltage" line.

- **11 (The Intuitive):** Integration means daily meditation to ground the "Static" of high-frequency intuition.

- **22 (The Master Builder):** Integration means thinking in "Decades" rather than "Days." You must never settle for small, petty goals.

- **33 (The Teacher):** Integration means service. Your lifestyle must include a component of mentorship, or your energy will turn inward and become self-destructive.

VIII. Navigating the "Vibrational Void"

There will be moments—usually during a **Personal Year 7 or 9**—where the numbers seem to go "Silent." You will feel like the blueprint has been lost. This is the **Vibrational Void.**

In a cohesive lifestyle, you don't panic when the void arrives. You recognize it as the "White Space" on the blueprint. It is the necessary silence between the notes of a song. When the math feels "dry," it is a sign that you have reached a plateau and are preparing for a vertical jump in consciousness. Use these periods for **Rest and Recalibration.**

IX. Conclusion: The Final Blueprint

You are no longer the person who started Chapter 1. You have built a bridge across the river of uncertainty. You have the formulas for your soul, the schedule for your success, and the ethics for your relationships.

The **Predictive Architect** does not fear the future, because they have already visited it in their calculations. They do not fear the past, because they have understood its lessons through the Pinnacles. They live in a vibrant, numerically-aligned **Present.**

The blueprint is in your hands. Now, go build the life you were calculated to lead.

Print and Keep Checklist: Daily Numerical Audit Tools

This final section is designed to be removed, printed, or digitally pinned to your workspace. These are the "Control Panels" for the **Predictive Architect.** Use them to ensure that the complex theories of the previous chapters are translated into the simple, disciplined actions that build a legacy.

In the architectural world, a structure is only as good as its maintenance schedule. Without a standardized way to check your alignment, the "Temporal Drag" of daily life will eventually pull you out of sync with your blueprint. By utilizing these checklists, you ensure that your 2026 launch—and the five-year plan that follows—remains mathematically sound and energetically vibrant.

I. The Morning Alignment Protocol
(The "First 60 Seconds")

Before you engage with the digital "noise" of social media or the reactive demands of your inbox, you must establish your vibrational coordinates. This protocol ensures you are not merely reacting to the world, but navigating it with architectural intent.

- [ ] **Step 1: Calculate the Universal Day**
  - *Formula:* Month + Day + Year (Current Calendar Date)
  - *The Logic:* This is the "Atmospheric Pressure." It tells you how the world at large is vibrating. If the world is in a **1 Universal Day**, expect high energy and a focus on "The New."
  - *Vibration:* ____

- [ ] **Step 2: Calculate Your Personal Day**
  - *Formula:* Your Personal Month + Calendar Day
  - *The Logic:* This is your "Personal Filter." It tells you how you will uniquely experience the global current. If your Personal Day is a **4**, you will feel a need for order, even if the world is chaotic.
  - *Vibration:* ____

- [ ] **Step 3: Perform the "Alignment Audit"**
  - Look at the relationship between the two numbers.
  - **Harmonic (Same/Complementary):** The path is clear. Push forward with maximum intensity.
  - **Dissonant (Clashing):** Example: Universal 5 (Chaos) vs. Personal 4 (Structure).
  - *Tactical Adjustment:* Acknowledge that you will need to exert more conscious effort to stay organized today. Build in a "15-minute buffer" for every task.

- [ ] **Step 4: Set the Tactical Intent**
  - Choose one primary objective that perfectly matches your **Personal Day**.
  - *Intent:* ________________________________ (e.g., "Today is a 3 Day; I will prioritize creative brainstorming over spreadsheets.")

II. The "Hour of Power" Quick-Reference Table

Do not leave high-stakes interactions to chance. Use this table to select the start time for meetings, contract signings, or major announcements.

The Formula: Personal Day + Current Military Hour = Personal Hour

If your Personal Hour is...	Use it for...	The Architectural Goal
1	**Initiation**	Launching a new idea; assertive requests; solo work.
2	**Collaboration**	Partnerships; sensitive discussions; listening; patience.
3	**Expression**	Marketing; presentations; social networking; joy.
4	**Foundations**	Signing legal contracts; bookkeeping; health audits; long-term building.
5	**Pivot/Action**	Sales calls; quick changes; travel; diversifying ideas.
6	**Harmony**	Family discussions; service; home matters; community building.
7	**Analysis**	Research; deep strategy; solitude; spiritual study.
8	**Manifestation**	Financial transactions; leadership moves; material gain.
9	**Completion**	Finalizing a project; closures; forgiving a debt; exit strategies.

III. The Weekly "Cycle Sync" (Sunday Evening SOP)

Architecture requires a "Site Survey" before the work begins. Spend 10 minutes every Sunday evening reviewing the upcoming seven days to proactively manage your energy expenditure.

- [   ] **The "Deep Work" Block (Day 7):** Identify any Personal Day 7s. Block off at least 2–4 hours for solitude. Guard this time fiercely; it is when your most profound architectural breakthroughs will occur.

- [   ] **The "Disruption Insurance" (Universal Day 5):** Identify days when the world is in a 5-vibration. These are "High-Volatility" days. Do not schedule back-to-back meetings. Keep your afternoon flexible to handle sudden pivots.

- [   ] **The "Social Expansion" (Day 3 or 5):** If you need to network or pitch a new idea, look for these days. The "Social Friction" will be at its lowest point.

- [   ] **The "Closure" (Day 9):** Use the final day of your 9-day sub-cycle to "clean the cache." Archive old emails, finish pending administrative tasks, and prepare the soil for the next Day 1.

IV. The Monthly "Pinnacle" Audit Checklist

At the end of each calendar month, you must zoom out to ensure you aren't "building in the wrong direction."

- [   ] **Pinnacle Alignment:** "Does my primary focus this month match my current 9-Year Pinnacle?" (e.g., If you are in a Pinnacle 8 but spent the month hiding away, you are out of alignment).

- [   ] **Resource Verification:** "Do I have the mental and financial 'Capital' to sustain next month's vibration?"

- [   ] **The Monthly "Pruning":** What one habit, project, or cost did I "End" this month (consistent with a Year 9 or Month 9 logic) to make room for new growth?

- [   ] **Goal Recalibration:** Based on the upcoming **Personal Month**, what is my primary "Key Performance Indicator" (KPI)?
    - *Next Month's PY Month:* ______________________________
    - *Next Month's KPI:* ______________________________

V. Relational Troubleshooting (The "Conflict Resolution" Toolkit)

When you feel friction with another person, do not react emotionally. Perform a **Vibrational Triage** first.

1. Calculate their Personal Day.
2. Calculate your Personal Day.
3. Analyze the Mismatch:
    - **If You are a 1 and They are a 4:** You are trying to move too fast for their need for structure. *Solution: Slow down and provide them with a detailed plan.*
    - **If You are a 7 and They are a 3:** You need silence while they need stimulation. *Solution: Communicate your need for withdrawal clearly so they don't take it as a personal rejection.*
    - **If You are an 8 and They are a 9:** You are trying to build more while they are ready to let go. *Solution: Negotiate a "Closure Phase" before starting the next venture.*

VI. The Predictive Architect's "Emergency" Toolkit

When things feel like they are collapsing, return to the math. It is the only objective anchor in a subjective world.

- **Feeling Overwhelmed?** Check if you are in a **Personal Year 5 or Month 5.**
    - *Action:* Simplify. Eliminate 20% of your non-essential tasks. Remind yourself: "This is a frequency of motion, not a permanent state of chaos."

- **Feeling Invisible/Stuck?** Check if you are in a **Personal Year 7 or 4.**
    - *Action:* Lean into the silence. Stop trying to force a "High-Visibility" result. Use the time for the "Library" or the "Wall."

- **Feeling Afraid of a Decision?** Check if the day is a **Personal Day 1 or 8.**
    - *Action:* If the vibration is high (1 or 8), the universe is giving you a "Green Light." The fear is biological; the opportunity is mathematical. Trust the number.

If you enjoyed this book, I'd greatly appreciate a review on Amazon because it helps me to create more books that people want. It would mean a lot to hear from you.

To leave a review:

1. Open your camera app.
2. Point your mobile device at the QR code.
3. The review page will appear in your web browser.

Thanks for your support!

Here's another book by Mari Silva that you might like

Your Free Gift
(only available for a limited time)

Thanks for getting this book! If you want to learn more about various spirituality topics, then join Mari Silva's community and get a free guided meditation MP3 for awakening your third eye. This guided meditation mp3 is designed to open and strengthen ones third eye so you can experience a higher state of consciousness. Simply visit the link below the image to get started.

https://spiritualityspot.com/meditation

Or, Scan the QR code!

Resource List

Overall Introduction

Books:

- **Heath, T. L. (1981).** *A History of Greek Mathematics: From Thales to Euclid.* Dover Publications. .

- **Jung, C. G. (1968).** *Archetypes and the Collective Unconscious.* Princeton University Press.

Online Sources:

- https://plato.stanford.edu/entries/pythagoreanism/

- https://archive.org/details/theonof-smyrna-mathematics-useful-for-understanding-plato

Book 1

Chapter 1

Books:

- **Balliet, L. D. (1917).** *The Philosophy of Numbers: Their Tone and Colors.* L.N. Fowler & Co.

- **Ore, O. (1988).** *Number Theory and Its History.* Dover Publications.

Online Sources:

- https://mathworld.wolfram.com/DigitalRoot.html

- https://nrich.maths.org/6546

Chapters 2 & 3

Books:

- **Aron, E. N. (1996).** *The Highly Sensitive Person.* Broadway Books.
- **Campbell, F. (1919).** *Your Days Are Numbered.* Richard R. Smith.
- **Tett, R. P., & Burnett, D. D. (2003).** "A Capacity-Based Model of Personality Trait Expression." *Journal of Applied Psychology.*

Online Sources:

- https://hsperson.com/research/
- https://www.psychologytoday.com/us/basics/big-five-personality-traits

Chapters 4 & 5

Books:

- **Csikszentmihalyi, M. (1990).** *Flow: The Psychology of Optimal Experience.* Harper & Row.
- **Baumeister, R. F., & Tierney, J. (2011).** *Willpower: Rediscovering the Greatest Human Strength.* Penguin Press.
- **Drucker, P. F. (1967).** *The Effective Executive.* Harper & Row.

Online Sources:

- https://www.authentichappiness.sas.upenn.edu/newsletters/internationl/flow
- https://hbr.org/2012/06/the-science-of-decision-making

Conclusion

Books:

- **Schrödinger, E. (1944).** *What is Life? The Physical Aspect of the Living Cell.* Cambridge University Press.
- **Adler, M. J. (1982).** *The Paideia Proposal: An Educational Manifesto.* Macmillan.

Online Sources:

- https://www.britannica.com/science/entropy
- https://criticalthinking.org/pages/the-role-of-socratic-questioning-in-thinking-teaching-learning/522

Reflection Questions

Books:

- **Bloom, B. S. (1956).** *Taxonomy of Educational Objectives: The Classification of Educational Goals.* Longmans, Green.

- **Mezirow, J. (1991).** *Transformative Dimensions of Adult Learning.* Jossey-Bass.
- **Jung, C. G. (1959).** *Aion: Researches into the Phenomenology of the Self.* Princeton University Press.
- **Ford, D. (1998).** *The Dark Side of the Light Chasers.* Riverhead Books.
- **Porges, S. W. (2011).** *The Polyvagal Theory: Neurophysiological Foundations of Emotions, Attachment, Communication, and Self-regulation.* W. W. Norton & Company.
- **Aron, E. N. (2010).** *Psychotherapy and the Highly Sensitive Person.* Routledge.
- **Senge, P. M. (1990).** *The Fifth Discipline: The Art & Practice of The Learning Organization.* Doubleday/Currency.
- **Paul, R., & Elder, L. (2006).** *The Thinker's Guide to the Art of Socratic Questioning.* Foundation for Critical Thinking.

Online Sources:

- https://cft.vanderbilt.edu/guides-sub-pages/blooms-taxonomy/
- https://www.instructionaldesign.org/theories/transformative-learning/
- https://www.psychologytoday.com/us/basics/projection
- https://jungiancenter.org/the-shadow-how-it-forms-how-it-works/
- https://www.polyvagalinstitute.org/whatispolyvagaltheory
- https://www.scientificamerican.com/article/sensory-processing-sensitivity/
- https://hbr.org/2015/01/the-authenticity-paradox
- https://criticalthinking.org/pages/the-role-of-socratic-questioning-in-thinking-teaching-learning/522

Book 2

Introduction

Books:

- **Deci, E. L., & Ryan, R. M. (1985).** *Intrinsic Motivation and Self-Determination in Human Behavior.* Plenum Press.
- **Goffman, E. (1959).** *The Presentation of Self in Everyday Life.* Doubleday.
- **Festinger, L. (1957).** *A Theory of Cognitive Dissonance.* Stanford University Press. **Jung, C. G. (1953).** *Two Essays on Analytical Psychology.* Princeton University Press.

- **Pink, D. H. (2009).** *Drive: The Surprising Truth About What Motivates Us.* Riverhead Books.
- **Maslow, A. H. (1954).** *Motivation and Personality.* Harper & Row.
- **Horney, K. (1950).** *Neurosis and Human Growth: The Struggle Toward Self-Realization.* W.W. Norton & Co.
- **Campbell, F. (1919).** *Your Days Are Numbered.* Richard R. Smith.

Online Sources:

- https://www.simplypsychology.org/self-determination-theory.html
- https://plato.stanford.edu/entries/self-knowledge/
- https://www.psychologytoday.com/us/basics/motivation
- https://www.nature.com/articles/s41598-021-00213-3
- https://hbr.org/2018/01/what-self-awareness-really-is-and-how-to-cultivate-it
- https://www.frontiersin.org/articles/10.3389/fpsyg.2020.00566/full
- https://www.apa.org/topics/personality/identity
- https://thesocietypages.org/theory/2012/03/12/erving-goffman-the-presentation-of-self-in-everyday-life/

Chapter 1

Books:

- **Deci, E. L., & Ryan, R. M. (1985).** *Intrinsic Motivation and Self-Determination in Human Behavior.* Plenum Press.
- **Mezirow, J. (1991).** *Transformative Dimensions of Adult Learning.* Jossey-Bass.
- **Jung, C. G. (1959).** *Aion: Researches into the Phenomenology of the Self.* Princeton University Press.
- **Porges, S. W. (2011).** *The Polyvagal Theory.* W. W. Norton.
- **Senge, P. M. (1990).** *The Fifth Discipline.* Doubleday.
- **Bloom, B. S. (1956).** *Taxonomy of Educational Objectives.* Longmans.
- **Campbell, F. (1931).** *Your Days are Numbered.* Richard R. Smith.
- **Lagerwerff, J. (1994).** *The Vowels of Your Name.* Blue Dolphin.

Online Sources:

- https://www.selfdeterminationtheory.org/
- https://www.psychologytoday.com/us/basics/motivation
- https://hbr.org/2018/11/what-is-motivation

- https://www.iep.utm.edu/pythagor/
- https://www.polyvagalinstitute.org/
- https://jungiancenter.org/
- https://cft.vanderbilt.edu/guides-sub-pages/blooms-taxonomy/
- https://www.instructionaldesign.org/theories/transformative-learning/

Chapter 2

Books:

- **Bloom, B. S. (1956).** *Taxonomy of Educational Objectives: The Classification of Educational Goals.* Longmans, Green.
- **Mezirow, J. (1991).** *Transformative Dimensions of Adult Learning.* Jossey-Bass.
- **Jung, C. G. (1959).** *Aion: Researches into the Phenomenology of the Self.* Princeton University Press.
- **Ford, D. (1998).** *The Dark Side of the Light Chasers.* Riverhead Books.
- **Porges, S. W. (2011).** *The Polyvagal Theory.* W. W. Norton.
- **Aron, E. N. (2010).** *Psychotherapy and the Highly Sensitive Person.* Routledge.
- **Senge, P. M. (1990).** *The Fifth Discipline.* Doubleday/Currency.
- **Paul, R., & Elder, L. (2006).** *The Thinker's Guide to the Art of Socratic Questioning.* Foundation for Critical Thinking.

Online Sources:

- https://cft.vanderbilt.edu/guides-sub-pages/blooms-taxonomy/
- https://www.instructionaldesign.org/theories/transformative-learning/
- https://www.psychologytoday.com/us/basics/projection
- https://jungiancenter.org/the-shadow-how-it-forms-how-it-works/
- https://www.polyvagalinstitute.org/whatispolyvagaltheory
- https://www.scientificamerican.com/article/sensory-processing-sensitivity/
- https://hbr.org/2015/01/the-authenticity-paradox
- https://criticalthinking.org/pages/the-role-of-socratic-questioning-in-thinking-teaching-learning/522

Chapter 3
Books:

- **Bloom, B. S. (1956).** *Taxonomy of Educational Objectives: The Classification of Educational Goals.* Longmans, Green.

- **Mezirow, J. (1991).** *Transformative Dimensions of Adult Learning.* Jossey-Bass.

- **Jung, C. G. (1959).** *Aion: Researches into the Phenomenology of the Self.* Princeton University Press.

- **Ford, D. (1998).** *The Dark Side of the Light Chasers.* Riverhead Books.

- **Porges, S. W. (2011).** *The Polyvagal Theory.* W. W. Norton.

- **Aron, E. N. (2010).** *Psychotherapy and the Highly Sensitive Person.* Routledge.

- **Senge, P. M. (1990).** *The Fifth Discipline.* Doubleday/Currency.

- **Paul, R., & Elder, L. (2006).** *The Thinker's Guide to the Art of Socratic Questioning.* Foundation for Critical Thinking.

Online Sources:

- https://cft.vanderbilt.edu/guides-sub-pages/blooms-taxonomy/

- https://www.instructionaldesign.org/theories/transformative-learning/

- https://www.psychologytoday.com/us/basics/projection

- https://jungiancenter.org/the-persona-how-to-use-it-without-being-used-by-it/

- https://www.polyvagalinstitute.org/whatispolyvagaltheory

- https://www.scientificamerican.com/article/the-science-of-first-impressions/

- https://hbr.org/2015/01/the-authenticity-paradox

- https://criticalthinking.org/pages/the-role-of-socratic-questioning-in-thinking-thinking-learning/522

Chapter 4
Books:

- **Bloom, B. S. (1956).** *Taxonomy of Educational Objectives: The Classification of Educational Goals.* Longmans, Green.

- **Mezirow, J. (1991).** *Transformative Dimensions of Adult Learning.* Jossey-Bass.

- **Jung, C. G. (1959).** *Aion: Researches into the Phenomenology of the Self.* Princeton University Press.
- **Ford, D. (1998).** *The Dark Side of the Light Chasers.* Riverhead Books.
- **Porges, S. W. (2011).** *The Polyvagal Theory.* W. W. Norton & Company.
- **Aron, E. N. (2010).** *Psychotherapy and the Highly Sensitive Person.* Routledge.
- **Senge, P. M. (1990).** *The Fifth Discipline.* Doubleday/Currency.
- **Paul, R., & Elder, L. (2006).** *The Thinker's Guide to the Art of Socratic Questioning.* Foundation for Critical Thinking.

Online Sources:

- https://cft.vanderbilt.edu/guides-sub-pages/blooms-taxonomy/
- https://www.instructionaldesign.org/theories/transformative-learning/
- https://www.psychologytoday.com/us/basics/projection
- https://jungiancenter.org/the-shadow-how-it-forms-how-it-works/
- https://www.polyvagalinstitute.org/whatispolyvagaltheory
- https://www.scientificamerican.com/article/sensory-processing-sensitivity/
- https://hbr.org/2015/01/the-authenticity-paradox
- https://criticalthinking.org/pages/the-role-of-socratic-questioning-in-thinking-thinking-learning/522

Chapter 5

Books:

- **Goleman, D. (1995).** *Emotional Intelligence: Why It Can Matter More Than IQ.* Bantam Books.
- **Porges, S. W. (2017).** *The Pocket Guide to the Polyvagal Theory.* W. W. Norton.
- **Mezirow, J. (1991).** *Transformative Dimensions of Adult Learning.* Jossey-Bass.
- **Bloom, B. S. (1956).** *Taxonomy of Educational Objectives.* Longmans.
- **Jung, C. G. (1959).** *The Archetypes and the Collective Unconscious.* Princeton University Press.
- **Salovey, P., & Mayer, J. D. (1990).** *Emotional Intelligence.* Imagination, Cognition and Personality.

- **Brackett, M. (2019).** *Permission to Feel.* Celadon Books.
- **Lagerwerff, J. (1994).** *The Vowels of Your Name.* Blue Dolphin.
- **Adler, A. (1927).** *Understanding Human Nature.* Greenberg.
- **Frankl, V. E. (1946).** *Man's Search for Meaning.* Beacon Press.

Online Sources:

- https://www.danielgoleman.info/topics/emotional-intelligence/
- https://www.polyvagalinstitute.org/
- https://www.psychologytoday.com/us/basics/emotional-intelligence
- https://hbr.org/2017/02/emotional-intelligence-has-12-elements-which-do-you-need-to-work-on
- https://www.yaleei.org/
- https://cft.vanderbilt.edu/guides-sub-pages/blooms-taxonomy/
- https://www.instructionaldesign.org/theories/transformative-learning/
- https://www.scientificamerican.com/article/the-science-of-empathy/

Conclusion

Books:

- **Campbell, F. (1931).** *Your Days are Numbered.* Richard R. Smith.
- **Jung, C. G. (1959).** *Aion: Researches into the Phenomenology of the Self.* Princeton University Press.
- **Csikszentmihalyi, M. (1990).** *Flow: The Psychology of Optimal Experience.* Harper & Row.
- **Porges, S. W. (2011).** *The Polyvagal Theory: Neurophysiological Foundations of Emotions, Attachment, Communication, and Self-regulation.* W. W. Norton.
- **Senge, P. M. (1990).** *The Fifth Discipline: The Art and Practice of the Learning Organization.* Doubleday.
- **Schwartz, R. C. (1995).** *Internal Family Systems Therapy.* Guilford Press.
- **Mezirow, J. (1991).** *Transformative Dimensions of Adult Learning.* Jossey-Bass.
- **Bloom, B. S. (1956).** *Taxonomy of Educational Objectives.* Longmans.
- **Jordan, J. (1965).** *Numerology: The Romance in Your Name.* DeVorss & Company.
- **Decoz, H. (1994).** *Numerology: Key to Your Inner Self.* Perigee Books.

Online Sources:

- https://www.selfdeterminationtheory.org/
- https://www.polyvagalinstitute.org/
- https://cft.vanderbilt.edu/guides-sub-pages/blooms-taxonomy/
- https://jungiancenter.org/
- https://thesystemsthinker.com/
- https://www.instructionaldesign.org/theories/transformative-learning/
- https://ifs-institute.com/

Reflection Questions

Books:

- **Paul, R., & Elder, L. (2006).** *The Thinker's Guide to the Art of Socratic Questioning.* Foundation for Critical Thinking.
- **Mezirow, J. (1991).** *Transformative Dimensions of Adult Learning.* Jossey-Bass.
- **Bloom, B. S. (1956).** *Taxonomy of Educational Objectives.* Longmans.
- **Porges, S. W. (2017).** *The Pocket Guide to the Polyvagal Theory.* W. W. Norton.
- **Frankl, V. E. (1946).** *Man's Search for Meaning.* Beacon Press.
- **Jung, C. G. (1959).** *The Archetypes and the Collective Unconscious.* Princeton University Press.
- **Argyris, C. (1990).** *Overcoming Organizational Defenses.* Prentice Hall.
- **Palmer, P. J. (2004).** *A Hidden Wholeness: The Journey Toward an Undivided Life.* Jossey-Bass.

Online Sources:

- https://criticalthinking.org/pages/the-role-of-socratic-questioning-in-thinking-thinking-learning/522
- https://www.instructionaldesign.org/theories/transformative-learning/
- https://www.polyvagalinstitute.org/
- https://cft.vanderbilt.edu/guides-sub-pages/blooms-taxonomy/
- https://www.psychologytoday.com/us/blog/the-unveiled-self
- https://www.yaleci.org/
- https://hbr.org/2018/01/what-self-awareness-really-is-and-how-to-cultivate-it

Book 3

Introduction

Books:

- **Dewey, E. R. (1971).** *Cycles: The Mysterious Forces that Trigger Events.* Hawthorn Books.

- **Campbell, F. (1931).** *Your Days are Numbered.* Richard R. Smith.

- **Gleick, J. (1987).** *Chaos: Making a New Science.* Viking.

- **Taleb, N. N. (2007).** *The Black Swan: The Impact of the Highly Improbable.* Random House.

- **Jung, C. G. (1973).** *Synchronicity: An Acausal Connecting Principle.* Princeton University Press.

- **Lagerwerff, J. (1994).** *The Vowels of Your Name.* Blue Dolphin.

- **Bunker, D. (2005).** *The Power of Personal Vibration.* Llewellyn.

Online Sources:

- https://www.foundationforthestudyofcycles.org/

- https://www.nature.com/articles/s41598-021-95444-y

- https://www.psychologytoday.com/us/basics/circadian-rhythm

- https://www.pnas.org/doi/10.1073/pnas.1718940115

Chapter 1

- **Books:**

- **Campbell, F. (1931).** *Your Days are Numbered.* Richard R. Smith.

- **Jordan, J. (1965).** *Numerology: The Romance in Your Name.* DeVorss.

- **Lagerwerff, J. (1994).** *The Vowels of Your Name.* Blue Dolphin.

- **Dewey, E. R. (1971).** *Cycles: The Mysterious Forces that Trigger Events.* Hawthorn Books.

Online Sources:

- https://www.foundationforthestudyofcycles.org/

- https://www.timeanddate.com/

Chapter 2

Books:

- **Campbell, F. (1931).** *Your Days are Numbered.* Richard R. Smith.

- **Decoz, H. (1994).** *Numerology: Key to Your Inner Self.* Perigee.

- Jordan, J. (1965). *Numerology: The Romance in Your Name.* DeVorss.
- Jung, C. G. (1959). *The Archetypes and the Collective Unconscious.* Princeton.
- Erikson, E. H. (1950). *Childhood and Society.* Norton.

Online Sources:

- https://www.psychologytoday.com/us/basics/developmental-psychology
- https://www.pnas.org/doi/10.1073/pnas.1718940115

Chapter 3

Books:

- **Campbell, F. (1931).** *Your Days are Numbered.* Richard R. Smith.
- **Decoz, H. (1994).** *Numerology: Key to Your Inner Self.* Perigee Books.
- **Gottman, J. M. (1999).** *The Seven Principles for Making Marriage Work.* Harmony.
- **Jordan, J. (1965).** *Numerology: The Romance in Your Name.* DeVorss & Company. **Vaughan, R. H. (1982).** *The Numerology of Relationships.* Para Research.

Online Sources:

- https://www.gottman.com/about/research/
- https://cycles.org/
- https://jungiancenter.org/jung-on-the-archetypes-of-the-collective-unconscious/
- https://www.psychologytoday.com/us/blog/stretching-theory/202305/the-psychology-of-the-similarity-attraction-effect

Chapter 4

Books:

- **Campbell, F. (1931).** *Your Days are Numbered.* Richard R. Smith.
- **Balliett, L. D. (1917).** *The Philosophy of Numbers.* L.N. Fowler & Co.
- **Lagerwerff, J. (1994).** *The Vowels of Your Name.* Blue Dolphin.
- **Avery, K. (1974).** *The Numbers of Life.* Doubleday.
- **Taleb, N. N. (2012).** *Antifragile.* Random House.

Online Sources:

- https://cycles.org/cycles-in-social-behavior-part-1/
- https://science.nasa.gov/resource/the-earth-calendar-and-planetary-cycles/
- https://papers.ssrn.com/sol3/papers.cfm?abstract_id=3135506
- https://www.timeanddate.com/time/about-utc.html

Chapter 5

Books:

- **Campbell, F. (1931).** *Your Days are Numbered.* Richard R. Smith.
- **Dewey, E. R. (1971).** *Cycles: The Mysterious Forces that Trigger Events.* Hawthorn Books.
- **Avery, K. (1974).** *The Numbers of Life.* Doubleday.
- **Rumelt, R. (2011).** *Good Strategy/Bad Strategy.* Crown Business.
- **Taleb, N. N. (2012).** *Antifragile.* Random House.

Online Sources:

- https://cycles.org/cycles-in-human-endeavor-the-9-2-year-cycle/
- https://hbr.org/2014/01/the-fallacy-of-the-five-year-plan
- https://papers.ssrn.com/sol3/papers.cfm?abstract_id=2656402
- https://www.timeanddate.com/date/leapyear.html

Conclusion

Books:

- **Campbell, F. (1931).** *Your Days are Numbered.* Richard R. Smith.
- **Duhigg, C. (2012).** *The Power of Habit.* Random House.
- **Avery, K. (1974).** *The Numbers of Life.* Doubleday.
- **Jordan, J. (1965).** *Numerology: The Romance in Your Name.* DeVorss & Company.
- **Clear, J. (2018).** *Atomic Habits.* Avery.
- **Taleb, N. N. (2012).** *Antifragile.* Random House.

Online Sources:

- https://www.gottman.com/blog/the-importance-of-empathy-in-relationships/
- https://cycles.org/cycles-in-human-endeavor/
- https://papers.ssrn.com/sol3/papers.cfm?abstract_id=2345501

Reflection Questions

Books:

- **Avery, K. (1974).** *The Numbers of Life.* Doubleday.
- **Campbell, F. (1931).** *Your Days are Numbered.* Richard R. Smith.
- **Decoz, H. (1994).** *Numerology: Key to Your Inner Self.* Perigee Books.
- **Gottman, J. M. (2011).** *The Science of Trust.* W. W. Norton & Company.
- **Senge, P. M. (1990).** *The Fifth Discipline.* Doubleday.
- **Whitmore, J. (2002).** *Coaching for Performance.* Nicholas Brealey.

Online Sources:

- https://www.gottman.com/blog/what-is-the-sound-relationship-house/
- https://cycles.org/the-art-of-forecasting/
- https://www.mindtools.com/pages/article/newTMC_05.htm
- https://onlinelibrary.wiley.com/journal/10990771

Overall Conclusion

Books:

- **Campbell, F. (1931).** *Your Days are Numbered.* Richard R. Smith.
- **Avery, K. (1974).** *The Numbers of Life.* Doubleday.
- **Decoz, H. (1994).** *Numerology: Key to Your Inner Self.* Perigee Books.
- **Clear, J. (2018).** *Atomic Habits.* Avery.
- **Taleb, N. N. (2012).** *Antifragile.* Random House.

Online Sources:

- https://www.gottman.com/blog/what-is-the-sound-relationship-house/
- https://cycles.org/cycles-in-human-endeavor/
- https://papers.ssrn.com/sol3/papers.cfm?abstract_id=3135506

Keep and Print Checklist

Books:

- **Campbell, F. (1931).** *Your Days are Numbered.*
- **Balliett, L. D. (1917).** *The Philosophy of Numbers.*
- **Clear, J. (2018).** *Atomic Habits.* .